Monkeys, Motorcycles, and Misadventures

A 3000 kilometre journey in Lord Hanuman's footsteps

HARSHA

ISBN 978-93-52013-77-7

First published in India 2015 by Frog Books
An imprint of Leadstart Publishing Pvt Ltd
1 Level, Trade Centre
Bandra Kurla Complex
Bandra (East) Mumbai 400 051 India
Telephone: +91-22-40700804
Fax: +91-22-40700800
Email: info@leadstartcorp.com
www.leadstartcorp.com / www.frogbooks.net

Sales Office:
Unit No.25/26, Building No.A/1,
Near Wadala RTO,
Wadala (East), Mumbai – 400037 India
Phone: +91 22 24046887

US Office:
Axis Corp, 7845 E Oakbrook Circle
Madison, WI 53717 USA

Editor: Cora Bhatia

Cover: Mistha Roy
Layout: Chandravadan R. Shiroorkar

Typeset in Palatino Linotype
Printed at Dhote Offset Technokrafts Pvt. Ltd.

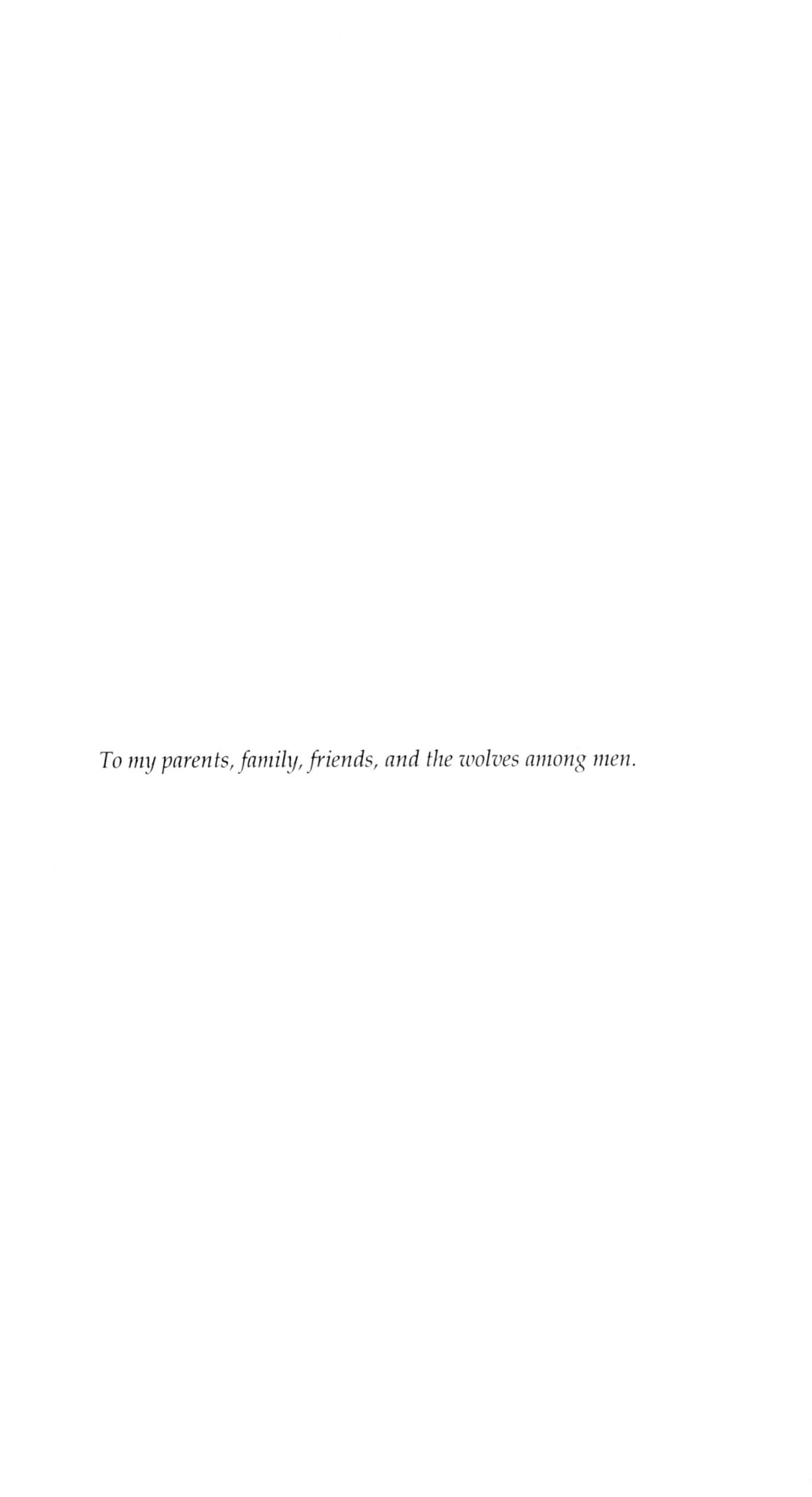

To my parents, family, friends, and the wolves among men.

CONTENTS

Prologue

I now knew what 'Tom' must have felt like at the end of an episode of 'Tom and Jerry'; every bone and muscle in my body hurt. My hands were so badly scratched that I couldn't touch anything without pain shooting up my arms. My stomach had shut down completely due to severe dehydration and my throat was so parched that it hurt when I swallowed. To top things off, I had probably fractured one of my ribs, ensuring that every step I took hurt like hell. My buddies, Sam and Sri, weren't doing all too well either.

How had it come to this? We had started off well enough, attempting a hard but doable day ascent and descent of Mount Mahendragiri in Nagercoil. Somewhere down the line though, we lost both our strength and our will. Now, all we wanted to do was get out alive.

We staggered down the mountain, too tired to even search for a trail. Thanks to the dehydration, we experienced raw thirst for the first time. At one point, we stopped next to a rock, which had a drop of water trickling down every five seconds and licked it for thirty minutes to sate our thirst. At another point, we found a pool of murky water with leaves, mud, and a decomposing prawn; what we did there is all but obvious.

We continued downhill, using every trick in the book to conserve whatever energy remained and get out before nightfall – jump, run, slide, rappel, and crawl. Ants, centipedes, and other insects crawled all over my body, biting down hard (I must have hit a nest somewhere), but I was too tired to react to the pain. I stumbled through thorns, without bothering to step away as they tore into my skin; I was…we were beyond caring.

While my exhaustion had numbed the physical pain, there was another kind of pain, one that I could not handle – a mental one, a voice in my head, which kept whispering that I would fail in what I set out to do - in fulfilling my dream, a dream that was eventually shared by Sam and Sri. It taunted me mercilessly and told me it was all over – that this was the end of the line.

The worst part was that the voice seemed to be right. We had run out of food and water several hours earlier and were exhausted to the point where we could only crawl forward. It was pitch dark, as we inched our way through the thorny shrubbery hoping not to run into any snakes or scorpions. We were several kilometres from civilization, that is assuming we were headed in the right direction through the forest; we weren't so sure anymore. There was no cell coverage in that area and since nobody knew where we were, the chances of someone coming to our rescue were minimal. In addition, all the beasts of the night would be up and about and looking for a meal.

Death seemed close. She had come close to collecting her bounty about half a dozen times already on this accursed mountain. Would she succeed in claiming us, I wondered. There was certainly no escaping her. It was only a matter of time; the only question was – was it our time now?

"I think I'm going to throw up thanks to your melodrama. Could you cut the crap and tell the story as it is," Sam said restlessly. "I don't want my epitaph to seem like an episode of *Kyunki Saas bhi bahu…*"

"He does overdo the storytelling sometimes. Doesn't he?" Sri added.

"Shut up. I'm telling the story and I will tell it the way I want."

I was about to start when Sam decided to cut in again, "Well, don't blame us later when people get bored of your inane rambling. Now get on with it already."

"Okay, fine! Here, let me start again 'I had a dream…'"

"Who do you think you are? Martin Luther King?"

"Shut up and let me start!" I said, now irritated at the repeated interruptions and the sarcasm. His words stung, even if that wasn't his intention.

"I had a dream in which I was travelling along the path Lord Hanuman followed in his search for Sita Devi, starting from Kishkinda (Hampi) through to Sri Lanka, visiting places related to the Ramayana like Anegondi, Hiriyur, Sirumalai, Madurai, Rameshwaram, Adam's bridge, Mount Mahendragiri, and Ussangoda along the way."

"Go ahead, don't leave out the clincher," Sam said.

"Well...I dreamt that I walked the route from Hampi, Karnataka all the way to Mount Mahendragiri near Nagercoil, Tamil Nadu."

"You knew that the distance from Kishkinda to Mahendragiri was around twelve hundred kilometres. You sold the idea to us saying it was a short hike, not a sixty-day cross-country trek. You suckered us," Sri said accusingly.

"Look at the bright side. The plan also involved catching a ferry from Tuticorin (Thoothukudi) to Colombo and then covering the two thousand kilometres in Lanka by motorcycle and **not** swimming or walking that distance as well. You know what that means – that we are done with the walking part, if we get out of this alive," I said with a smile, which wasn't well received by either of them.

"You and your stupid dream are what got us into this situation in the first place. Did we really have to climb up this godforsaken mountain?" asked Sam.

"We have to follow our dreams in order to achieve true happiness. The world would definitely be a happier place if everyone did."

"Why don't you go to sleep and dream of Hawaii? I always wanted to go there," Sri said with a grin.

"If you don't follow your dreams, you will end up following someone else's," I continued.

"I had a dream that I was kicking your ass, doing that would truly make me happy. Want to make me happy?" Sam said, returning my smile. It was the first time I had seen him smile all day. Definitely not a good sign considering he was usually smiling.

"If one advances confidently in the direction of his dreams, and endeavors to live the life he has imagined, he will meet with a success unexpected in common hours." - Henry David Thoreau

Considering our situation, the fact that we were sitting there and joking might be considered extremely foolhardy, but it was all we could do to keep our spirits up and hopefully get out alive. We had been in tight spots before, but this was probably the worst we had ever gotten ourselves into; we were in way over our heads. How in the hell did we end up here and what had we done to mess up so badly? Everything seemed to be going along so well just a few days earlier.

Maybe I should start from the beginning. I was going through a particularly difficult phase in my life when I had the dream for the first time. Isn't it odd how most stories have this in common? Maybe because faith is tested and strengthened during tough times. Anyway, I digress.

In the dream, I saw *myself* walking along a road, entering a temple and offering prayers to Lord Hanuman. As I watched *myself,* I heard *my* thoughts about how *I* was walking along the route taken by Lord Hanuman and how it was destined and that it all made sense. It was strange to hear myself think from an external perspective, but since the dream was so *simple,* I didn't take it too seriously. It was only when I had the same dream again, a few days later that I realised it wasn't random and that it meant something. What it was though, I wasn't sure at that point of time.

I talked to Sam and Sri about it, but they weren't sure about what it meant either. What they knew for sure was that they weren't walking halfway across the country, based on a random dream. In fact, even I wasn't sure if I should start walking based on a dream, especially since I was leading a comfortable life with a stable job, a house, and other material comforts. Was I willing to sacrifice all that I had, just to pursue a dream? It was extremely tough to choose between staying in my comfort zone and venturing out into the unknown in the pursuit of a dream.

The comfort zone offered security, stability, and above all, a sense of belonging. On the other hand, I felt that unless I pursued my dream, I was missing out on something big. It could have been God offering me a chance (at least that's what I hoped the dream was). Could I just ignore it? I was confused and afraid, but figured that facing my fears and insecurities, and moving forward was all part of the plan. It took me a long time to convince Sam, Sri, and more importantly, myself that it was more than just a dream, that it meant a lot more. How much more was something I couldn't even imagine at that point of time, but we would all find out later.

After thinking through and struggling for such a long time on the decision, I assumed that explaining the trip to my family and friends would be an easy task. It wasn't! I was met with plenty of raised eyebrows and questions regarding my mental state when I told them of my plan. The discussions to convince my family and friends started calmly, but quickly turned nasty. I was accused of running away from responsibility and of having no real understanding of what I was doing - both by people who didn't know me and by people who were close to me and cared. We stoically weathered the storm of accusations and insults and by the end of it, we received plenty of support from everybody – family, friends, acquaintances, and as we found out later, even complete strangers!

PART – 1: Hope

"Faith is taking the first step even when you can't see the whole staircase."

— Martin Luther King Jr.

D-Day minus 8 months: It does not do to leave a live dragon out of your calculations, if you live near him.

Eight months before we started the trek, I decided to nail down two important tasks. Firstly, I had to identify the *Hanuman route* as accurately as possible and come up with a route map for our journey. Secondly, I had to list out all the equipment required for the trip and figure out a way to get it.

To come up with the route map, I read books, scoured the internet, and spoke with various people to find places associated with the legend of Lord Hanuman or the Ramayana. After my research, I marked the route out and decided to have a simple conversation with the lads to discuss it, but a conversation with them was never going to be simple.

"I have picked up a few maps and have charted out a route for us to follow," I said, placing the map before them.

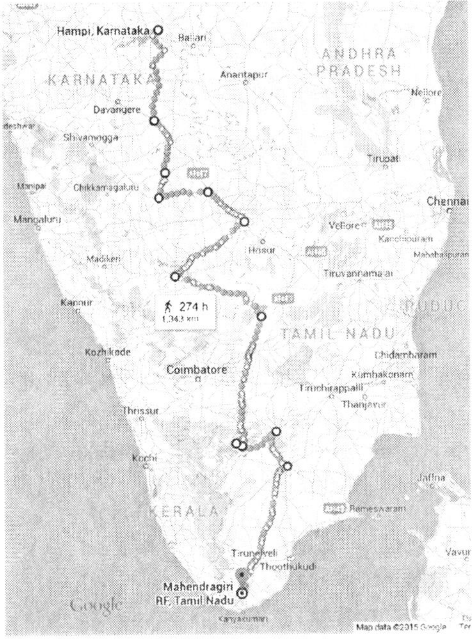

"The route follows the path taken by Lord Hanuman and passes through various places associated with Lord Hanuman and the Ramayana. We will start from Hampi and walk all the way to Mahendragiri. From there, we will head to Tuticorin and catch a ferry to Colombo. Once in Colombo, we will rent a motorcycle, stock up on supplies, plan our route, and drive around. Simple eh?" I ventured, encouraged by the fact that they hadn't said a word in opposition yet. That's when my luck ran out, along with their patience.

"I remember the last '*simple*' plan you came up with that involved motorcycles. Manali to Leh, remember?" Sam burst out in anger.

"Let me list out what went wrong on that trip – for starters, you didn't get the papers for the motorcycles and the cops detained us for almost half a day at the state border, then one of the motorcycles stalled and we couldn't do anything because you got the wrong tool kit...."

"Ok. I get it. I get it," I said, trying desperately to interrupt the conversation.

"Wait. I'm not done yet. Then our motorcycle's tyre had a puncture and we couldn't fix it because we had the **wrong** tool kit, then your motorcycle stalled, because you forgot to fill engine oil, then we realised that we had no money because you forgot to withdraw money from the ATM before we started riding and the altitude sickness..."

"That was great planning, oh wise and fearless leader!" Sam said, ending his long rant.

"You remember that, right? Now ask yourself why you remember it. Let me tell you why – it's because we faced a series of seemingly insurmountable challenges, but we persisted and finally came out on top. If it was a walk in the park you wouldn't even remember it," I said, trying to defend myself.

"And the implication being that we are going to get screwed. I have no clue why I humour your stupidity," Sam continued. He could be relentless at times.

Thankfully, Sri came to my rescue, "Relax guys. What's the

worst that could happen?" He on the other hand never seemed to worry about anything.

"More importantly, what about other places that are off our planned route? I want to visit Coorg, Rameshwaram, and Kanyakumari among other places," Sri continued.

"Let's walk along the *Hanuman route* and for any off route places we want to visit, we can catch a bus to the place and return to the route after visiting the place. Happy?" I asked, hoping to close the discussion quickly.

"Happiness isn't good enough for me! I demand euphoria!" Sam said, quoting Calvin, in his snarkiest tone. At times, I hated the guy. It was funny when his sarcasm was directed at other people but when it was directed towards me, I hated it.

"Since we are going to be walking a long way, we also need to decide on the gear we need to carry," I said.

As soon as the topic shifted to gear, Sam and Sri brought out the *gospel of Ultralight Backpacking*. "The weight of the backpack is inversely proportional to the level of enjoyment on a trip," ministers Sam and Sri, of Church Ultralight, crowed triumphantly, and all was good. They were fanatical about the whole Ultralight backpacking nonsense.

The Ultralight school of backpacking essentially stated that backpackers should carry as light a load as safely possible. Generally, this meant carrying a total backpack weight of less than 10 Kgs including shelter, food, and water. However, for extreme ultralight nuts like Sri and Sam, this meant doing month long trips with a daypack and making lemming–like decisions while packing.

Their pantheon of Gods included Ray Jardine, (who wrote the ultralight gospel, '*Beyond Backpacking*', and thru hiked the Pacific Crest Trail and the Appalachian Trail multiple times) and Emma "*Grandma*" Gatewood, (an early pioneer of ultralight-*ing*, who hiked the Appalachian Trail {~3,500 km} at the sprightly age of 67. She was the first woman to do the trail and did so with only shoes, a shower curtain, and a laundry sack filled with a few other accessories).

Going by Sam and Sri's backpacking rules, I wasn't allowed to carry 'unnecessary junk' like a *tablet computer*, multiple pairs of clothes and underwear or heck even a full tube of toothpaste. "It weighs too much, besides a full tube of toothpaste is unnecessary," they said. If it wasn't on the *Ten Essentials*, it wasn't needed, they said in unison. After several calm discussions with Sri and not so calm discussions with Sam, we finally agreed upon the following gear:

1. *Navigation:* Maps (Karnataka and Tamil Nadu state maps and detailed district maps), compass, and GPS unit (GPS in India is iffy especially in rural areas and forests).
2. *Shelter:* Bivy sack and space blankets.
3. *Food and water:* Peanut butter, protein bars, MREs, and iodine pills (to purify water). We planned to pick up extra food and water wherever we passed through villages/towns.
4. *Clothes*: Cap, jacket, two shirts, two pants, innerwear, and shoes/socks.
5. *Headlamp / flashlight:* Petzel Tikka headlamp.
6. *First aid kit:* Standard kit with antiseptic, bandages, and medicine.
7. Matches and a lighter.
8. *Knife:* Gerber serrated edge knife.
9. *Toiletries*: Soap (one-half), toothbrush and paste (again one-half), deodorant (they only agreed to let me carry this as it would double up as a "flamethrower" and hence could be categorised under 'emergency safety equipment') and sunscreen.
10. *Safety:* Pepper spray for protection against bears and elephants in a worst-case scenario. Animals never behave the way animal experts or movies predict they will.

Deciding on the equipment was half the battle, getting it together was the other half. We had some of the gear with us already from our previous treks, but getting the rest of it was a hassle as it wasn't available in India. We had to order it online and attempt to get it through the usual networks of relatives, friends, relatives of friends, and friends of relatives of friends.

In the meantime, we went through additional sources of information (more books, people, and the Internet) to finalise the route. This was when we came across the following theories regarding the location of *Lanka*:

1) Theory 1 (our current route). *Lanka* from the Ramayana is present-day Sri Lanka and Kishkinda is present-day Hampi (this is the most widely believed theory).
2) Theory 2: *Lanka* is present day Maldives (or somewhere close by).
3) Theory 3: *Lanka* is located in India, south of the current Vindhya mountain range, past a large river possibly the Godavari. Other possible locations ranged from Orissa (Sonepur – surrounded by a river) all the way to Assam
4) Theory 4: *Lanka* was an island off the coast of Andhra Pradesh/Orissa, which subsequently sunk, similar to Atlantis. This would match many of the criteria for *Lanka*. I had heard rumours of such an island from several people, but with no real evidence, we decided it was better to let sleeping dogs lie.

Based on the verses written in the *Valmiki Ramayana*, we knew that the Monkey King Sugreeva had detailed knowledge of the geography of the land. He gave precise directions to his monkey troops of the location of *Lanka* including various landmarks like rivers, forests, peaks, and kingdoms. Keeping these landmarks in mind, we looked at the various theories and found that Theory 1 seemed to be the one that was the most relevant.

Key factors that supported the first theory were geographically accurate landmarks from the *Ramayana* like Rama Setu, Hampi (Kishkinda), and the Cauvery River, *Lanka's* description as an island, the Mahendragiri and Trikuta peaks and the presence of whales off the coast of *Lanka* (Mirissa).

There were a few factors that conflicted with this theory though; the major one being *Lanka's* width mentioned as 100 *Yojanas* (~800 miles), whereas Sri Lanka was only ~180 miles wide. It was impossible to establish conclusively that Sri Lanka and *Lanka* were the same, but it still looked like our best bet.

Eventually, we decided to follow the route based on the assumption that *Lanka* was Sri Lanka and focus more on the experience rather than on getting the route to 100% geographical or historical accuracy. We hoped that we would get additional information as we progressed.

D-Day minus two days: Run to the hills

It was almost time. We had two days left to the start of our trek from Hampi. Over the past few months, we managed to get all the gear together including the half bars of soap and half the tube of toothpaste. I did question Sam and Sri's sanity over the practice, but considering that I was dragging them along for a 1200-kilometre trek based on a *dream*, I realised that I was in no position to be judgmental.

We had decided to do the trek in four legs, with three to four day breaks between each leg, to allow for any adjustments in gear and for recuperation. Details of the legs are as follows:
Leg 1: Hampi to Bengaluru (~350 kilometres) with a break at Bengaluru
Leg 2: Bengaluru to Tirupur (~400 kilometres) with a break at Coimbatore
Leg 3: Tirupur to Nagercoil (~450 kilometres) with a break at Kanyakumari
Leg 4: Sri Lanka (~2000 kilometres on a motorcycle)

To kick off the trip, we planned to catch a train to Hospet and then head over to Hampi. Most of my family and friends called me before we set out; it was apparent they were worried, but nobody asked us to stay. Sometimes, being a stubborn ass had its perks.

Though we all had butterflies in our stomachs, it wasn't because we were worried about the trek; it was more out of nervous excitement. This was something we had looked forward to for a long time and now it was *go time*. Since we were feeling quite restless, we double-checked our maps, gear and even hoisted the bags on our backs to check the weight distribution and adjust the straps.

Suddenly, Sam looked at me and asked, "Can you go into the kitchen and get me something please?"

I naively walked in and asked him what he wanted.

"Can you see the refrigerator?" he asked.

"Yes, what do you want from it?"

"Oh. Is it still there? I thought you packed it in here by mistake!" came his reply.

"For once I agree with him. What do you have in the backpack? I thought that we agreed to keep this light," Sri said.

I started listing out what I had packed, "Well I have the Bivy (1 Kg), Food (5 Kgs), equipment (camera, GPS, chargers ~1.5 Kg), water (2 litres which is ~2 Kgs), books (1 Kg), clothes (1 Kg) and water filter (2 Kgs)."

"Every Kg counts in long trips and you are definitely carrying 5 Kgs extra, which you need to cut out. Look at that filter, why do we need a water filter when we have the purification tablets?" Sam asked.

"That's because water purification tablets are known to have side effects, if used frequently," I replied.

"Okay fine. Let's look at all the food you are carrying – 'Ready to Eat' meal packs, glucose packs, energy bars and what's this... **condensed milk**?" Sam said, sighing in exasperation. "Didn't you forget the Junior Horlicks powder and the tea and biscuits? That way, we can have a tea party every day. What the hell dude! Trust me! We are far more likely to die in a road accident than through starvation." Those words would come back to bite us in the ass later.

Sri decided it was time to impart some of his infinite wisdom, "A man can survive without food for fifty days, without water for five days, without oxygen for five minutes, but not even for five seconds without hope! With all that baggage, I have no hope." The guy loved quoting things he had read or heard and it didn't help that he twisted it to his advantage most of the time.

I tried to take control of the situation before it escalated. "Listen, we are going to consume the food as we travel, so the pack is going to get lighter. It weighs around 13 Kgs now, just 3 Kgs more than what we planned, but it is going to get lighter," I pleaded.

"Easy for you to say. I know that Sri and I will end up carrying your load anyway!"

"I still think we could use the extra food."

"Food is fairly easy to find when you are walking in South India. There are villages every few kilometres, so you are never far from a decent meal," Sam interrupted.

"That's true. Do you remember when we trekked up Skandagiri and found a tea shop on the top of the hill?" Sri asked, effectively closing the argument.

I had no choice but to dump a lot of food; food that we could have used later in the journey, especially when we were close to dying on Mahendragiri, but we will get to that later.

Day 1: Monkeywrenching with Smith and Hayduke

Location: Hampi, Karnataka

We reached Hospet in the morning and headed over to Hampi. Hampi was the capital of the 14th century Vijayanagar Empire and is a UNESCO World Heritage site. The remains of the once magnificent empire spread over a vast area and offered plenty of interesting places to visit. In addition, *Kishkinda*, the capital of the *Vanaras* (monkeys) is believed to have been located in and around Hampi.

We decided to start our journey, with a visit to Anjana Parvatha, which according to legend is the birthplace of Lord Hanuman. A temple dedicated to Lord Hanuman on top of the hill, marked out his birthplace. The hill was barely three hundred metres high and yet the climb left me exhausted; a fact that made me nervous, considering the magnitude of the journey ahead of us. Once at the top, we caught our breath and took in the amazing view of the surrounding areas. All around us, there were hundreds of boulders and rocky hills with green valleys and we could imagine the hordes of monkeys that must have once run amok all over these hills.

We entered the temple and prayed to Lord Hanuman to give us strength and watch over us, as we attempted to follow in his footsteps. After that, we headed towards the Vittala temple, which was located across the river Tungabhadra, from Anjana Parvatha. The temple is dedicated to Vittala, an *avatar* (divine form) of Lord Vishnu and was built in the 16th century. It is considered an architectural masterpiece for its Mandapas, intricate carvings, frescos, and the exquisitely sculpted stone chariot. The architects, who built the temple, carved out huge stone pillars to function as musical instruments. When the pillars are struck, they produce musical notes depending on the instrument they represented (Wind, String or Percussion instrument). These pillars were placed in a specific order to allow musical pieces to be played. In the past, the temple itself functioned as a stage, with musicians using the pillars to perform concerts.

While the Vittala temple is the most renowned of the collection of monuments at Hampi, there are several other monuments worth seeing. We visited the Queen's palace, the Zenana enclosure, Lotus Palace, Elephant stables, Pushkarani, Lakshmi Narasimha temple and finally ended up at the Virupaksha Temple.

The rain came pouring down, forcing us to slow down, and appreciate the architectural wonder that was the Virupaksha Temple. It had the most exquisite carvings on the walls and murals of Lord Vishnu and Lord Shiva. We took a walk around the temple compound and to our surprise came across a chained elephant.

"Oh great! Another destroyed life. Why do many temples capture and keep these wild animals? How is oppression acceptable in a place of worship?" Sam spat out with venom.

"Are you referring to the elephant? Temple elephants are supposed to be treated royally," Sri replied.

"'*Supposed to be,*' being the key words. They are wild animals and we are taking away their freedom and enslaving them. For what? For God? You really believe God would want that?"

"While they might restrict the elephant's freedom, they get plenty of food and are practically worshipped."

"I would rather live free, as a pauper than a constrained life as a king."

"So, I take it you love your job," I chipped in, to return the favour for the last few days.

"Your grave - thousand dogs - full bladders - visit," was his reply.

By the evening, we had finished our tour of Hampi and settled into our small hotel room for the night. Thoughts fill empty spaces and since my mind was completely blank, dark thoughts started to fill it, especially one nasty thought, which insisted that I would die! Doubt and panic set in and I wasn't excited about the journey anymore. The sheer volume of the task ahead and the innumerable things that could go wrong dawned on me – we had to walk nearly twelve hundred kilometres through unknown terrain, oppressive weather, and with very limited knowledge of the local language (Kannada and Tamil). My vocabulary was limited to a few words in Kannada and the grossly stereotypical Tamil phrase 'Yenna Rascalla'. Impossible as it might seem, Sri and Sam were worse off in the language department and could practically be considered mute!

Would we be able to complete the journey? Was I in any position to even attempt it in all honesty? Was it worth the risk? These and a thousand other doubts plagued me. I had never attempted anything of this magnitude earlier. What would happen if we fell sick or had an injury along the way? Our knowledge of first aid was rudimentary consisting only of means and methods to make ourselves go numb; heck, if we were ever injured, the only thing we could probably do was drink copious amounts of alcohol to numb the pain! These and a thousand other doubts raced through my mind.

At first, I tried to counter my doubts, but quickly realised it was an exercise in futility. Battling self-doubt is like fighting a hydra – no sooner than you cut off one "doubtful" head, two more heads take its place! To overcome self-doubt you either had to:

A) Have a clear plan in place that addressed all concerns (yeah right! We barely had a semblance of a plan).

B) Acknowledge its presence and have the will power to ignore it completely (what is this will power you speak of and where can I buy some?)

C) Create circumstances in which backing off is not an option.

Luckily, for me, I didn't need to create them; circumstances already dictated that it was too late to back off. I had committed almost everything to this journey. I had left my job, family, and friends behind. I had told everyone that I was doing this and set out. Everyone believed in me and I couldn't let them or myself down. I had no option, but to ignore the doubts in my head and move forward. I convinced myself that it was all planned and that I could handle it, if any problems cropped up.

I tried to grab some sleep to steady my nerves and to ensure an early start, but that wasn't meant to be. It's funny how your mind responds to uncertainty. Mine, kept throwing up images of my legs being blown up by dynamite. I didn't know what to make of it, when I suddenly realised that we were near the mining empire of the Reddy brothers, so I guess my mind was subconsciously telling me to watch where I stepped. Perfect dreams for a perfect location!

Day 2: Common sense...tingling

Location: Hospet, Karnataka

They say that a journey of a thousand miles begins with a single step, usually an unforgettable one. Ours was unforgettable as well, albeit for all the wrong reasons. We woke up early, packed, and thought that it would be a good idea to test the pepper spray that we were carrying. It was a particularly strong one, specifically designed to deter bears and I was nominated to carry out the testing by an overwhelming majority.

Here's a piece of advice – if you are about to do something and a voice pops up in your head saying, "That's a bad idea," please listen to it. Let me elaborate – I held the can near the window, aimed it outside, and tried to spray a little bit, just to check if the spraying mechanism worked. Precisely at that moment, there was a sudden gust of wind, which blew everything back into the room and straight into my face. A second later, my eyes started burning and it felt as though my face was on fire. I ran towards the bathroom and splashed plenty of cold water on my face and eyes to reduce the burning sensation, but to no avail.

A few minutes later, the fumes entered our lungs and we started coughing and sneezing violently. With no other option, we ran out of the room and shut the door behind us. Since we had left the window open, we figured that the spray would dissipate in fifteen to twenty minutes and headed downstairs to have breakfast. By the time we were back, people across the entire floor were coughing and looking for whoever was responsible! That was our exit cue. We quickly entered our room, picked up our gear (thankfully it was all packed), ran downstairs, paid the bill, and left; luckily for us, no one decided to check our room when we checked out. It was a close call, since we certainly didn't want to start our journey from a police station! Sri wasn't too happy about leaving the mess behind, but with no means to clean it up or explain how we had managed to do something so stupid, we decided that making a silent exit was the better option. (Yes, we were all great big scared-cats.)

The adrenaline from the incident blanked my mind out and I started the trek without much thought. After around twenty minutes, the adrenaline faded, rationality returned, and I had a panic attack. I could clearly feel my racing heart and the butterflies in my stomach. I attempted to continue walking forward, but couldn't move thanks to my trembling legs. A wave of nausea swept over me and I felt incredibly weak. All this while, my brain was screaming at me to go home, back to safety and comfort. I tried to calm down but just couldn't manage it. Sam and Sri just watched silently; they knew better than to push me forward. Stressing out a cornered, scared animal is always a horrible idea.

After what seemed like an eternity, I somehow managed to convince my brain that the walk wouldn't kill me. I told myself that at the first sign of trouble, I would quit immediately. I gathered my resolve, steeled myself, and started walking. Taking that first step was probably the hardest thing I ever did in my life, but once I started walking, the nervousness faded away.

We entered the coordinates we had mapped into the GPS and it threw back a bunch of directions, which we followed diligently. My face still stung from the pepper spray and washing it didn't help either. The jerks just laughed at my misery and made bad puns. Well, the next time something needed to be 'tested', it wouldn't be me doing it.

Apart from that, everything seemed to be going surprisingly well, which was never a good sign. I checked the GPS and noticed something strange; it was pointing in the direction we had come from! This was when we realised that the GPS was displaying units in HMS mode and we had entered the coordinates in HM mode. We had wasted well over an hour walking in the wrong direction! After wasting an additional thirty minutes tinkering with the settings on the GPS device, we managed to fix it and finally started walking in the right direction.

The route ran along sandy flats with little vegetation, except for the odd shrub. It was dull, drab, and dusty and yet it did little to stifle our excitement. Every step was an experience and as we looked across the arid plains, we felt like cowboys exploring the Wild West albeit without the horses! We watched in wonder as dust devils swept across the barren land and lizards scampered across the sands to evade their wrath. While it was very sunny, our sense of adventure overcame any thoughts about the weather and we eagerly moved forward, taking in the sights and sounds.

By 12 noon, we had walked around twenty kilometres at an average pace of five km/hr and were twenty-two kilometres from our planned stopover for the night – Kudligi. The pack weighed heavily on my back and shoulders, but it wasn't a hard walk, as it was mostly flat ground. Since we were making good pace, we slowed down a little and decided to take in the experience. The change in attitude probably made us more approachable because people started walking up to us and began conversations. They were curious about the fools walking in the middle of nowhere and thought we were mad for walking instead of taking a bus. Oh well, one man's dream is another man's madness.

Along the way, we visited several temples including a couple of ancient Shiva and Vishnu temples that were being restored by the Archaeological Survey of India (ASI). None of them offered any insights into Lord Hanuman's journey though. This however changed when we came across two old Hanuman temples near Kudligi. The locals believed that the *Vanara Sena* (Monkey army) led by Angada and Hanuman passed through this area in their search for Sita Devi. We went inside the temples, saluted the Monkey God, and prayed for his blessings.

While stepping out of the last temple, I tripped over a stone and staggered onto the road. As I picked myself up, I saw Lord Hanuman inches away from my face! The Hanuman in question was stickered on the front of the vehicle that had stopped right in front of me. I just stood there in amazement until the person driving the vehicle spoke up.

"Are you coming along?" the stranger asked, completely out of the blue.

"Now that's what I call divine intervention!" Sri exclaimed.

"Divine intervention? Are you daft? I call it creepy as hell. In all seriousness, are we going to accept a ride from a total stranger? He could be a psychopathic axe murderer for all we know," Sam whispered to us.

"Oh come on! Have some faith. We are walking along Lord Hanuman's path to Lanka, we stepped out of his temple, and now a person who has the Lord's image on his vehicle is offering us a lift. This has to be divine intervention," Sri countered.

"I guess you are right," I said hesitatingly. Even though I said it, I wasn't completely sure what to make of the situation.

"Trust me on this, guys. We generally don't trust a lot of people who genuinely want to help us. Why? It is because we tend to exaggerate the few bad incidents that we have experienced. It is flawed human logic and a horrible assessment of risk probabilities. Out of ten people we meet, six want to help, three don't care, and one might have bad intentions. That being the case, why shouldn't we trust the vast majority? Travel with an open mind and have more faith is what I say."

"Fine. I'm not inclined to listening to you ramble on and besides, I'm not going to look a gift horse in the mouth," Sam whispered.

Since we were all in agreement, we thanked the stranger and accepted his offer.

"On the way, let me show you the Marulasiddeshwara temple in Ujjini," the stranger said.

"That's odd. Did we mention that we were visiting temples to him?" Sam asked, clearly surprised.

Sri was clearly excited, "Dude, do you now believe that this is divine intervention? There was no way he could have known that!"

The stranger drove us around for a long time, even though the GPS indicated that Kudligi was only five kilometres away from where he had picked us up. Since we had decided to trust in what Sri called divine intervention, I turned off the GPS and tuned into what the stranger was saying. Throughout the drive, he spoke of various temples in that area, his crops, and his kids.

An hour later, we reached the Marulasiddeshwara temple and after a quick visit, we continued our drive. The stranger eventually dropped us off at Jagalur and asked us to head to Chitradurga. We considered giving him money for taking us to the temple and driving us around, but we did not want to offend him or the gods with such materialistic offerings. Instead, we gave him some chocolates, which we knew would put a smile on his kids' face and thanked him with genuine smiles.

It was impossible to make sense of the incident. Sri insisted it was an act of God, a gift for our earlier kindness (we had helped a guy with a punctured tyre that morning) and more importantly – a sign. Sam thought it was just a coincidence. As usual, I was confused and no matter how much we discussed it, my confusion remained intact. That's the way faith works I suppose, we interpret incidents in a way that matches our beliefs.

We caught a bus to Chitradurga and checked into a hotel for the night. Word of advice – never stay at a hotel of recent construction. While the rent might be cheaper, the service and amenities are bound to suck, as it happened in our case.

Day 3: Live together, die alone

Location: Chitradurga, Karnataka

The next morning, I took the lead as we started walking. We hit the highway and walked for a couple of kilometres, when Sam exclaimed, "Aren't we going in the wrong direction? Why the hell are we going back to Kudligi?"

"Yes, we did pass through Kudligi, but we weren't walking. I want to walk the entire way, so we are heading back to Kudligi and will resume walking from there," I replied.

"What? That doesn't make sense. I thought you agreed when I said that meeting the stranger was divine intervention. Don't you believe that it was divine intervention for us to end up here?" Sri asked.

"Fuck that. Tell me what this is all about? This is not just about a dream, is it? I followed you on this journey without any questions. I knew there was something more to it than your supposed dream, but I didn't press you on it. I need to know now though, because going back all the way to Kudligi, just to "walk" through it doesn't make any sense. Why are you hell bent on walking the entire distance?" Sam asked.

"Leave it. It's late already and we have a long way to go, so let's start walking," I replied, hoping that they would shut up and follow me.

That however, wasn't meant to be. For once Sri was in agreement with Sam, "I am not walking anywhere without getting some answers. If we are doing this together, we need to know what's on your mind and what this is really about."

"Really? Are we doing this now?" I asked, with an exasperated sigh.

"I'm not going anywhere unless you give me a reason. It's your call hero," Sam shot back.

"I'm afraid..." I replied after a while.

"Afraid? Are you serious? Of what?" they asked in unison.

"I'm afraid that if I don't walk the entire route, I'm never going to get my faith back."

"What the hell are you talking about? What faith?"

I took a few minutes to figure out how best I could explain my situation. I had hoped not to have this conversation, but now it seemed as if there was no way to avoid it. It was all Sri's fault, if we had not taken the stranger's help, we wouldn't be in this situation. I cursed myself for accepting his dumbass logic about "divine intervention" and wondered why I agreed with him in the first place. Whatever be the case, I realised that they needed to know the truth. Even if I could avoid telling them the truth at that point of time, I knew that I would have to do it eventually. There was no escaping it, so I might as well get it over with, was what I thought.

"My faith…in God and people. Something has changed over the last few months. Whenever I look around, all I see is people being greedy, selfish, all-round assholes. Sometimes, I think that nobody cares anymore, not even God. Ever since I can remember, I always had my faith and it has kept me going and helped me deal with shit like this. Now, I seem to have lost my faith and that has left me confused and scared."

"Welcome to the club of loving misanthropes! In all seriousness though, when did you lose your marbles?" Sam asked.

"It's been this way since my grandma passed away, a year back. I am not saying that the world has become a bad place. I know it hasn't changed, it's my perspective that has."

"How is faith related to this? Faith in what, exactly?" Sri asked.

"Look, my dad is very religious and when I was young, he taught me to have faith in God. As kids grow up, they start to question their faith, go through a process of discovery, meet new people, have experiences, screw up, do the right things, and eventually sort their faith out.

However, in my case, I never questioned my faith in the first place. I never needed to, because my grandma always shielded me from doubts about faith. She always reminded me to look at the bright side of things and seek out the goodness in people.

In her own way, she was always there to counter any doubts and insecurities. After she passed away, I started seeing things differently; I saw how good people struggled and suffered, while jerks thrived. Earlier I never noticed these things, but now I do and I wonder if anyone gives a shit. I have serious questions about my faith in God and humanity and I am looking for answers."

"I know you spent a lot of your childhood with your grandmother and loved her a lot, but you have to understand that life goes on," Sam said.

"I had no idea it was affecting you this much. It is normal to question your beliefs, when you face difficulties. I have been through a similar phase and I can tell you that it will pass. Time heals everything," Sri added.

"No. You don't understand how I feel. I feel cynical and jaded because I don't have faith in anything or anyone anymore and as a consequence even seemingly insignificant things piss me off now. I'm angry most of the time, everything, and anything gets to me. All this anger, it's consuming and makes me question things even more."

I know I'm going down a slippery slope, but I can't stop thinking this way and frankly, it scares me. I have tried to keep my thoughts under control, but it isn't working so this is my last option. I'm basically clutching at straws here, but I believe I had to get away, to experience a world different than my own and hope that it helped me find some answers and regain my faith. Tall ask, I know, but my faith is what has driven me, strengthened me, kept me in one piece, and made me who I am. I wouldn't be the same without it. I just want to believe. That's all I ask for."

"What if you find out that there is no such thing?" Sam asked.

"Then I'm just going to have to accept the fact that my entire outlook towards life was built upon a falsehood, and deal with the consequences, however harsh they may be."

"And the dream. Was it a lie?"

"No. It was real and that is the only reason why I think this might work. It's my one chance at getting my faith back, but I have to do it perfectly, every step of the way."

"Listen, we trusted you and followed your dream so have some faith in us. Don't just walk back because you are scared or confused. The walking, in itself is not going to answer any of your questions. You need to trust in God and walk with an open heart," Sri said.

Listening to Sri, Sam went back to business, "Look at Robin Sharma go! Seriously though, we are going to stick with you, even if you want to do something stupid like walking back to Kudligi!"

"Just look for the signs, believe, and follow," Sri continued.

"Guys, I think I need some time to think this through, if this even makes sense."

I spent an hour there on the highway, thinking about it, but couldn't come to any conclusion. I realised that standing there and beating myself up wasn't going to help things. What I needed was faith and a whole lot of it to take my next step. How ironic was it that on this long journey to regain my faith, one of the first steps itself involved taking a leap of faith! Sri and Sam figured that visiting a temple might help me get my perspective in order. It looked as if they were committed to the trip come what may.

We caught a bus to Davangere to visit the Shamanur Anjaneya temple. It was a small, yet famous temple, established by Vyasaraja Swamy around nine hundred years ago, and had a huge statue of Lord Hanuman at the entrance. There was a bunch of people present, even though it was quite early in the morning. Watching people pray in the early hours should have strengthened my faith and my resolve; it didn't. My head was filled with more doubt than ever before. I slinked away to a corner and sat there thinking. These guys must have sensed it because they left me alone to sort myself out. I sat there for a long while, but still couldn't arrive at any solution to my dilemma.

What happened next is rather unbelievable – a monkey ran past me and stopped at the temple door. It then looked back at me and ran out of the temple. Was that a sign? I ran out after it and looked around but couldn't see him. Was I hallucinating? Had the previous day's walk tired me out so much? I honestly couldn't tell, but since I wanted to *believe* and get my faith back, I decided to take this as one of those *signs* that Sri kept talking about and go forward with as much faith as I could muster. Sometimes that's all you need in life, a small push in the right direction.

The idiots were happy about my decision and we caught a bus back to Chitradurga. Chitradurga is an old town known chiefly for its huge fort located atop a rocky hill. Since we had time to kill, we headed to the fort. It was built during the 17th and 18th centuries by a series of rulers from the Rashtrakuta, Nayak, and Chalukya Nayak dynasties. The fort had seven layers of defensive walls and resembled a giant snake coiled around a hill, thanks to the walls. It was so huge that it took us three hours to explore the important sections of the fort. There were a couple of magnificent temples within the fort and the view from the top of the hill was superb.

As we walked out of the fort, we discussed how awesome it would be to witness a real battle, with an army laying siege to this magnificent fortress, especially considering its near impregnable defences. Apart from the seven layers of defensive walls, the fort had multiple moats, invisible passages with traps, secret exits, narrow corridors with defensive positions, and hundreds of watchtowers.

"Now that we are done with the fort, I want to meet Kothi (Jyothi) Raju," Sam said, as soon as we stepped outside.

"I think he is here only on Sundays," I said.

"Why the hell can't you plan anything right? The guy can climb the walls of this fortress like only a monkey can and is one of India's best rock climbers. It's like meeting Chris Sharma or Alex Honnold," Sam screamed at me.

"I'm sorry, but I genuinely forgot."

Sri decided it was time to quote Mahatma Gandhi, *"Freedom is not worth having if it does not include the freedom to make mistakes."* He could be a lifesaver at times, mostly because he drew away Sam's ire.

"I've had it with you. The only thing you can do is quote other people. Can't you come up with something original?"

"All my best thoughts were stolen by the ancients," was his response, this time quoting Emerson.

"We need to get this asshat a lobotomy, pronto."

Day 4: Clint Westwood: Sharpest gun in the East

Location: Chitradurga, Karnataka

In the morning, we started towards Hiriyur, diligently following the path indicated by the GPS. Along the way, we ran into a villager near an old Hanuman temple, at D.S. Halli. He walked with us for the next five kilometres and we communicated through a combination of hand signs, Hindi, Kannada, and English.

As we walked, he asked us if we could get him a job on the contract that we were here to work on. We had no clue what he was talking about, so we told him that we were just passing through. We continued walking and ten kilometres ahead, we ran into two locals, who were also looking for work. This continued for a while, with several other people asking us the same thing. It turned out that they had heard of a contract for a new road or something similar and hence had come here in search of a livelihood.

I used to complain that my work was not fulfilling and that it did not pay enough, but it was only when I met these people that I realised that work was a privilege and of the value it held. While I was working in IT, I took it for granted and didn't realise what it had given me – something to look forward to every morning, a task to accomplish and when the day was done, something to look back on with satisfaction and pride.

I learnt the hard way that a job done diligently (no matter how trivial or boring it appeared) was something that could always provide joy and a sense of achievement.

"Once you decide on your occupation... you must immerse yourself in your work. You have to fall in love with your work. Never complain about your job. You must dedicate your life to mastering your skill. That's the secret of success... and is the key to being regarded honourably." - Jiro Ono

We continued walking and at around lunchtime, met a goatherd resting under a tree. We sat for a while under the same tree wondering what to do for lunch, when suddenly the goatherd opened his lunch pack and offered to share it with us. We could see that he barely had enough for himself, yet he offered it to us. The unexpected act of selflessness on a tough day brought a tear to my eye, but I quickly wiped it away before Sam noticed it. (He would have a field day making fun of me if he noticed!)

Since the goatherd was particularly insistent, we ate a small portion of his meal and offered him some money, which he vehemently refused. So instead, we gave him some chocolate bars.

"Do you see the goodness in people now? If this isn't proof enough, what is?" Sri asked, as we walked onward.

"Screw that. Does our hero think he is Santa Claus? He has given away almost all of our chocolate bars already. We need to save some of them for emergencies. You can only be so nice to the world, be too nice and the wolves will rip you apart," Sam said.

"The hardest thing to do is give when you have the least, and this person offered us whatever little food despite knowing that he would go hungry. It was the least we could do in return," I countered.

"I agree. See kid, there is so much good in people. We tend to lose sight of that in the mad rush of daily life, or in your case through anger and sadness," Sri said.

"You have *goat* to be kidding me!" Sam replied.

"That pun was *Baaa*d!" Sri retorted.

The puns kept flowing for quite a while after that. That was how it was with these guys, one minute they fought like cats and dogs and the next they made bad puns and laughed. I wasn't complaining though, at least it helped keep my spirits up and distracted me from the god-forsaken heat.

A little ahead, we ran into another person who thought we were walking because we couldn't get a lift. I guess he didn't believe that anyone in their right minds would voluntarily be walking in the ridiculous heat. We tried to tell him, through whatever little Kannada we knew, that we really wanted to walk, but I guess the message was lost in translation. Taking pity on our condition, he decided to take matters into his own hands and teach us the fine art of flagging a vehicle down.

Learning the art, involved a three-step process that was apparently easy to learn, but took a lifetime to master. Step one – stand on the side of the road and face the traffic in the direction we planned to go. Step two – "identify" a target vehicle that was at least one hundred and fifty feet away. Step three – hold our palms face down parallel to the ground and move them up and down slowly, as if we were patting a kid on the head.

"So I take it we are officially members of club *Pedobear* now that we know the secret hand sign!" Sam commented in his usual snarky manner.

"Oh come on. He was trying to help us…" Sri said.

"…get into jail," Sam said, cutting in.

"Pawsibly."

"Honestly, you are un*bear*able."

"Bear puns now. Really guys?"

We stopped at a roadside dhaba for lunch and a police officer sitting there eyed us warily. I gave him the best, innocent smile I could manage, praying that he would pay us no heed.

"Good job hero. I think the smile worked. I am sure he is thoroughly convinced that you need to be in a special needs program," Sam said.

"I will be happy as long as this doesn't turn out like the "police encounter" during our previous trek," Sri replied.

The encounter Sri referred to, took place a few years earlier while four of us were hiking in the Western Ghats in Karnataka. We had climbed a mountain called Kumara Parvata and spent the night on the summit. The next day, we descended the mountain from the other side and ended up in a small town at the base of the hill. We then entered a shady bar & restaurant and ordered lunch. While waiting for our food to arrive, we spread a map across the table and tried to identify a trail for the next section of our hike.

After a few minutes of loud and intense discussion, I went to take a leak when a random guy stepped up to the urinal next to mine. After his offer to shake my hand over the urinal separator went unrequited, he went about asking me a bunch of questions, "What was my name? Which city do I come from? Where was I going?" and so on so forth. Since I was busy doing my business, I grunted a few one-word replies and eventually told him I did not speak Kannada.

As if that wasn't weird enough, when I returned to our table, we noticed several people enter the restaurant, sneak glances at us, and walk into an adjacent room in the place. After twenty minutes of this weird behaviour, two men appeared at the entrance of the place. One of them stayed near the door and the other headed straight towards us and announced that he was a policeman. He told us to raise our hands and surrender quietly, since they had the restaurant surrounded and there was no chance of escape!

We were shocked and had no clue of what was happening. All of us panicked and started blabbering explanations, while desperately trying to make sense of the situation. After listening to our pathetic and incoherent jabber for a few minutes, the cop took pity on us and curtly explained the situation. Apparently, some over enthusiastic folks in the restaurant saw us and figured we were terrorists plotting a major attack. It seems, the vigilant folks in that fine town also panicked after looking at our shabby clothes, backpacks, maps, and GPS devices and promptly called the cops. (To add context, this was just a few weeks after the horrific attack in Mumbai, where a few terrorists had sneaked in and started shooting civilians).

After explaining the situation, the cop asked us to show our IDs. We fished out our driver's licenses, which the cop examined closely (I had a nasty feeling that the first thing he checked were our names, to make sure that we weren't Muslims). After being somewhat convinced of our innocence, he looked at the door and nodded his head towards another cop, indicating that all was clear. It was only then that the other cop sauntered in, looking like a classic Bollywood hero in his black baggy pants and silk shirt. Turned out that the guy was the police inspector and for all his macho looks, he had sent a poor constable inside to check on us, while he stayed near the door (probably to make sure his ass was safe, if we really were terrorists with guns and bombs).

After checking our IDs and bags multiple times and forcing us to answer all sorts of personal questions, they eventually let us go with whatever little dignity we had left (which was none). We silently walked out of the restaurant towards the bus stand, while what seemed to be the entire town stared down the 'terrorists'. If looks could kill, we certainly would be dead. We cursed the stupid people and their stupid mob mentality under our breath, but were thankful for having escaped with our lives instead of being strung up to some random tree.

Coming back to the current story, we got out of the dhaba without incident and continued walking. Walking in these parts should have been easy due to the flat terrain, but that wasn't the case, thanks to the raging heat. The sun kept draining us out and no matter how much water we drank, it was never enough. After a couple of hours of walking, we finally reached Hiriyur and checked into a lodge, but not before we learnt another lesson – never ever ask an auto-rickshaw driver to take you to a good lodge or hotel; you will either (A) get fleeced or (B) end up at a sleazy place. Since we had the luck of the devil, we checked positive in both those aspects! A better option would have been to ask the owner of a *paan* shop or teashop for help.

Day 5: Whaddya' mean it's too hot there? Get back here, and I'll warm up your milk for you, cry-babies!

Location: Hiriyur, Karnataka

After spending a restless night at the lodge in Hiriyur, we woke early the next morning, and checked our maps for our planned route (Hiriyur > Huliyar > Tiptur > Dabaspet > Bengaluru). We started towards Huliyar to visit the Sri Dasharatha Rameshwara Sri Kshetra temple, as there were stories connecting this temple to the Ramayana. Legend has it that this was the place where King Dasharath received the curse, which led to his son, Lord Rama's *Vanvas*.

The story goes like this – King Dasharath had been out hunting in the jungle and heard some rustling in the bushes. He believed it to be an elephant and immediately shot an arrow into the bushes, hoping to hit the animal. The arrow found its mark. Unfortunately, it was not an elephant in the bushes, but a young boy named Shravan who was collecting water for his old, blind parents.

In a final act of love, the dying boy requested the King to take some water to his parents, as he did not want them to remain thirsty. King Dasharath, being an honourable man, went to the boy's parents and confessed his mistake. The boy's father was overcome with grief and cursed the king to undergo the same suffering that he unwittingly thrust upon them, that of losing a son. Several years later, the curse took effect and King Dasharath was forced to exile Lord Rama for fourteen years. The story goes on to say that King Dasharath, overcome with remorse, had a Shiva temple built at the spot where he killed the boy. The legend also states that Lord Rama visited this temple before starting his exile.

From our reading of the map, we thought the temple was close to Hiriyur, but after considerable confusion and chaos, we found out that it was actually closer to another town called

Hosdurga. Once we reached Hosdurga, we asked some folks about the temple, but our limited knowledge of Kannada ensured that we were directed to an altogether different Shiva temple, called the Halu Rameshwara temple.

The visit to Halu Rameshwara temple was quite unremarkable except for one disgusting part, when the priest stood **in** the *Teertha* pool filled with rotten channa, bananas, flowers, plastic and other waste, picked up some prasad from the same pool and asked us to have it. We later found out that the Prasad *miraculously* appears in the temple pond and that each type of Prasad has some significance associated with it. What I got was some channa and a rotten banana. I was wondering how people could blindly believe and eat the Prasad they receive from the pond, when they could clearly see all the rotten eatables and plastic waste being thrown in and floating around, right in front of their eyes.

At that moment, I realised the irony of the situation. Here I was, looking down upon people and their 'blind faith', when I was guilty of the same crime. Blind faith is what got me in this situation in the first place! I had always blindly believed that God took care of everything in the world and had built a utopian version of the world inside my head, all the while remaining blissfully oblivious to everything that contradicted my ideas. When I finally started *seeing* things differently, my world came crashing down.

Standing near the temple pond and questioning how someone could have "blind faith" gave me an important insight – that while one can have faith, one also has to question it. Blind faith is more dangerous than having no faith. It was what had gotten me into this situation. Now, I was questioning it, refusing to accept irrationality. Would my newfound rationality help get my faith back or would it prove to be too huge an obstacle, I wondered.

The Oxford dictionary defines faith as "*Strong belief in the doctrines of a religion, based on spiritual conviction rather than proof,*" and here I was, looking for proof contrary to the definition of faith itself. Would I get any proof and what would I do once I got it? I didn't even know what "proof" I was looking for. I decided to follow the golden principle of "I don't know what I am looking for, but I will know it when I see it," and moved ahead.

We got back to Hosdurga, readjusted out bearings, and after a further four hours of torture under the harsh sun, finally reached the Dasharatha Rameshwara temple. As we entered the temple complex, the first thing we noticed was a cliff face on the left and a pool of crystal-clear water below it. The inner sanctum of the temple was located in a cave on the other side of the pool. The temple complex had many trees, which provided respite from the harsh sun. The odd sunbeams that managed to sneak through the thick tree cover reflected off the pond's surface giving it a mesmerising glow. A troop of boisterous monkeys, playing all over the cliff face, only served to make the scene more amazing. The tranquillity of the place refreshed us and brought us renewed energy after a long, tiring, and frustrating journey. The only thing that marred an otherwise perfect scene were the few pieces of trash that floated on the surface of the pond.

That was enough, to get Sam started, "People can be so callous, even in the abode of a God they fear."

"Fear is an unusual choice of words. Wouldn't you rather have said respect or love?" I asked.

"Nope. I will go with fear. Many people pray simply because they are afraid – of facing life and its challenges. That is why you see them praying only when they face difficulties. If it wasn't fear they would pray at all times."

"I think you are forgetting about the millions of people who serve God by working in places of worship, like the one we are standing in right now. It's not fear that drives them, it's faith," Sri said.

"In these days, faith is a lot to expect from people, even from those that serve God. God would have to be a personal miracle dispenser for people to truly *believe*," Sam responded dryly. "Heck, look at our own hero. He wants proof from God to believe in him."

"Sometimes your cynicism surprises me. I wonder if YOU need this trip more than I do," I said.

"I accept reality and not the dream world that both of you fools seem to live in. We are as strong as we make ourselves, not as strong as someone decrees us to be."

"It's called faith. You wouldn't understand, you barbarian," Sri said. His anger was evident from the way he said it.

"Listen you arrogant douche. I have had enough of your self-righteous attitude and talk. I have been through far worse than you can even imagine, so shut up."

"Yeah, I'm sure you suffered a lot, while you were getting that fancy degree of yours and as you sat in your AC office all day."

"I practically raised myself and it wasn't God or faith that got me through; it was my own strength. If you want anything done, you had better be strong enough to do it yourself. That's something you couldn't possibly comprehend, apple polisher."

This was now getting personal. I had to step in before things got out of hand, "Knock it off gremlins. We have a long walk ahead of us."

They did shut up, but the tension between them was electric and all I could do was wait until they calmed down. We went through a quick puja and returned to the village. It started to drizzle by the time we started our long walk to Huliyar. We had to cover around twenty-five kilometres in four hours of sunlight – a bit of a push but certainly manageable. Both of them remained silent throughout the walk and the silence only made the journey seem longer.

By the time we reached Huliyar, it was 7 p.m., and the rain was pouring down. Huliyar was a tiny town, more of a village actually. There were hardly any shops around and our chances of finding a place to stay seemed bleak. We asked around town and ended up at the only lodge in town. It was an old, dirty looking building, seemingly straight out of a *Ramsay* brothers' film. As if that wasn't creepy enough, the "manager" stood outside the building gleefully stroking his long beard, in the pouring rain with nary a second thought.

"Hello. Could we get a room please?" I asked.

The manager looked at me in an amused manner and replied, "Yes. It's Rs. 200 for an hour." We should have figured out the scene right then, but in our defence, we were tired and completely drenched.

"We need it for the entire night."

"Oh! In that case it will be Rs 300," replied the manager, clearly surprised.

"Uh. Is this a shady place?" Sri asked innocently.

That was all that Sam needed to pounce on him. "Duh! What do you think genius? Oh, wait. Do you even think?"

All of a sudden, Sri started chanting, "Remember the black kitten. Remember the black kitten...."

"What the hell are you talking about? Are you on drugs? Can I have some?"

In the meantime, the manager decided he needed to reassure us, "Yes. Yes! Very decent. No police raiding!"

"Dear God!" was all that Sri said.

"What the hell!" I exclaimed.

"I think I will kick him in the nuts. That would be poetic!" Sam said.

Since this was the only lodge in town, I figured we should take a look at the room "Guys, we don't have a choice. Let's go up and have a look at the room. It can't be that bad. Right?"

It was. The room exceeded our worst expectations, shat all over the concept of expectations, and lowered the global threshold for them, all in one cursory look. It was so bad that a disease would have caught something in that room. The floor was littered with dirt, cigarette butts, spittle, the bed dirty from God only knew what, and I could swear I saw semen marks on the walls and the ceiling! Yes on the bloody ceiling! The room stank of alcohol, vomit, sweat, shit, piss, and every other imaginable bodily fluid. In the infinitesimally remote chance that someone still didn't get it, there was a packet of 'Dreamz' in the window and an empty liquor bottle. If ever a lodge deserved the title '*lodge*', this was it.

The manager took note of our reactions, as we picked our jaws off the floor and offered us the room at a discounted price of Rs. 200. Sounds great huh? We got a discount in a shady lodge. We were so lucky! Since we definitely needed a place to sleep and I needed to charge my camera, we eventually accepted his offer.

As soon as we entered the room, we swore a blood oath that if any of us touched anything inside the room, even accidently, the other two would immediately kill that person, wrap the body in plastic sheets to contain the "infection" and proceed to burn the body in an isolated area to prevent an epidemic. Watching all those Zombie movies was definitely educational.

Sleeping on the footpath outside would definitely have been a better and cleaner option. The only upside was that the lodge was very silent. However, that changed at around 10:30 p.m., when all hell broke loose. We heard moaning, shrieking and grunting from the adjacent room. It stopped after ten minutes and then started from the room on the other side. We realised that we were not going to get any sleep that night. The only good that came out of that fiasco was that both Sam and Sri focused on the room, rather than on each other.

Day 6: The Pilbara Wanderer

Location: Huliyar, Karnataka

By 5 a.m., we were out of the lodge without any sticky issues. Thirty-eight kilometres to Tiptur with an early start was going to be a walk in the park, or so we thought. The first fifteen kilometres went by easy and we even had a dog walking along with us for a few kilometres.

The dog reminded me of a dog I had when I was a kid – a Labrador mutt. She had an uncanny sense of direction and could find her way home from anywhere. She once went with my dad to a place around fifty kilometres away, somehow managed to get loose, and decided to take a walk. My dad came home that evening thoroughly exhausted after having searched for many hours to find her, only to find her sitting on the porch, wagging her tail!

"OH BOY OH BOY OH BOY OH BOY OH BOY OH BOY! I had a grand adventure today. Where were you hooman? You missed it. I found this strange fish, then I smelt ten dog butts, pissed on eight cars, ate some poo, and then I found this big pool of mud.....DID I TELL YOU I LOVE YOU I LOVE YOU SO MUCH YOU ARE MY BEST FRIEND."

Man, I could definitely have used her sense of direction on the trip. That wasn't a possibility though since she had passed away several years earlier. Thinking of her reminded me of the sharp stab of pain I felt when my parents broke the news to me. Not really an appropriate memory considering the situation. In any case, she was the last pet I ever had.

After around twenty-five kilometres of walking, Sam started to get the feel of the trip, at least the pain part of it. Sri and I noticed that he was walking with a slight limp and wondered if he would hold up until the end of the leg. The strain of walking in the hot weather was definitely catching up to us. Despite his struggle, he did not say a word and stoically plodded on. That was just the way he was, silently toughing out any task demanded of him.

He hadn't had it easy growing up. Sam lost his mother in a fire accident when he was eight and was raised by his father. A kind and friendly man, who more often than not let Sam do his own thing. Since Sam was on his own most of the time, he developed a strong independent streak. He saw it as a weakness and personal failure to depend on anyone. This *tough guy* persona of his was always a pain to deal with though. Take the current situation. Even though he was struggling to keep up with us, we were helpless. We thought about reducing our pace and making it easier for Sam, but he glared at us silently daring us to say or do anything that would even remotely be considered as "helping" him.

At this point, we ran into a villager who asked us what we were doing. We had noticed over the past few days that people from villages were extremely curious and friendly. I guess we would be too, if we had time to kill. We explained to him what we were doing and he asked us if he could walk with us for a while. A very odd request, because in the past when we told people the purpose of our travel, they would look at us as if we were escapees from an institution. However, this stranger seemed to be totally cool with whatever we were doing and with him keeping us company, it helped Sam push through the last few kilometres into Tiptur relatively quickly.

Tiptur is a major commercial centre for Tumkur district and it showed from the sheer number of shops and marketplaces. Since we had only passed through villages and small towns for the last few days, we were surprised by how crowded and polluted Tiptur was. There were just so many people!

We checked into a lodge, a proper one, but its owner was a pain and reminded me of what I was trying to avoid – arrogant and greedy people who could die any second, but still wanted to earn money at any cost, even their soul. Maybe they thought that they could buy a soul later with all the money they earned. They were similar to people, who disregarded their health to earn money and later spent all their money trying to recover their health. Oh well, to each his own.

Day 7: Everybody be cool, this is a robbery!

Location: Tiptur, Karnataka

The next morning, we visited the Kote Anjaneya Swamy temple, an ancient temple that was established in the Krishna Deva Raya Era (~1500 CE) by the king's mentor, Vyasaraja. It is located in a narrow street near the bus stop and was nearly empty during our visit. Praying in peace was the best thing we could hope for in a temple, something we had learned to appreciate, thanks to all the offbeat temples we were visiting. After a quick puja, we decided to take a bus to Tumkur (back to the original route) and start walking from there. At the bus stop, we ran into a frail old woman who was begging for money.

Sri offered her some money saying, "Please take this mother."

We were all shocked by her reaction; tears welled up in her eyes immediately and her earlier stoic face changed to a mixture of grief, anger, and joy. She said something on the lines of, "My son…something…something," blessed Sri, and walked away. We boarded a bus silently and sat down, but what we had experienced wasn't something that we could have ignored easily.

I was the one who broke the silence, "It's pretty sad isn't it? That old woman can barely stand on her feet and yet she has to beg in this hot sun to survive. All my life I have taken what I had for granted and spent so much time trying to get more rather than being satisfied with what I had, and sharing it with the less fortunate. I feel like a monster."

"Don't beat yourself up. Most people are inconsiderate, selfish, and corrupt and would rather hoard money for their great grandchildren, rather than help the poor. Welcome to the real world kiddo," Sam said in his usual cynical manner.

"Yeah right! It's always someone else's fault. I don't see **you** helping out people daily. So get off your high horse and stop blaming others. There are plenty of people, who do their bit to help. You don't hear about them only because they don't do it for recognition," Sri countered.

"That's the problem. Isn't it? We have been led to believe that when we do something good, it has to be kept under wraps or you lose the whole sanctity of it. I say – brag, make a show of it, and raise hell. Only when you show it off, will others be inspired to join in. When doing something good, to hell with modesty is what I say. Heck, when I won Rs 30,000 in a tournament, I gave it all away to charity, and I told the entire world about it."

Sri was smiling as he said, "If I didn't know you better I would have called that bragging."

"Sarcastic bitch. You are like the proverbial crab in the bucket," was Sam's response.

"I agree with Sam on this. Even if one person gets inspired or guilt tripped into helping, it would be worth it. So let's all make one hell of a show of whatever good we do."

After a couple of hours on the bus, we were in Tumkur where we had lunch and started walking towards Dabaspet. We had eaten or given away a lot of food that we had originally packed and were carrying very little water. My backpack was definitely a couple of kilograms lighter, yet it felt as if it was getting heavier with each step. I stopped and readjusted all the straps to even out the weight distribution. That helped for a grand total of five minutes after which it started wearing me down again.

I realised that it was because of the hot sun, which was sapping all my energy. The weather was getting hotter by the day and at this rate, we would melt down during one of these walks. Heat exhaustion was now our biggest threat, so we tried to keep ourselves cool by pouring water over our caps and wrapping wet handkerchiefs around our heads. It was all in vain, as the sun would evaporate the water in a matter of seconds. The ideal solution was to walk only in the mornings and evenings and avoid the hot afternoons, but that was impractical since we planned to walk around forty kilometres every day.

After a long five-hour walk, we reached Dabaspet and proceeded towards Sivaganga. The Sivaganga temple is located on a hill nearly fourteen hundred metres high with four faces, which *apparently* resemble Nandi, Ganesha, Cobra, and a Shiva Linga. The temple is dedicated to Lord Shiva and is famous for a phenomenon in which ghee applied to the *Linga,* quickly turned into butter. Unfortunately, we couldn't witness this miracle as the temple was being closed for the evening.

Apart from the temple itself, also to see there are the *Patala Gange, a Nandi* statue, and the *Olakala Teertha.* The *Olakala Teertha* is an underground spring that can only be seen through a hole in the rocky ground. Apparently, only the *'blessed'* could touch the spring water through the hole and hence there was a long line of people, waiting to check their *'blessed'* rating.

Since I was now looking at things from a rational point of view, it was surprising to see how people kept grasping at straws and trying to find miracles (**where there weren't any to be found**) instead of opening their hearts and praying. I mentioned it to the guys, only to have Sam rudely point out that it was similar to what I was doing.

The best part of the entire temple visit was the troop of monkeys, which ruled over the temple and its surrounding areas.

"Notice how the monkeys run a thriving extortion racket? Every visitor has to *donate* fruits or groundnuts if they don't want to be harassed by these monkeys," Sam said.

"This bunch seems like real bullies. Everybody is paying the *Monkey Tax,*" Sri observed.

"Let's just sit here for a while and watch. It's entertaining watching animals bullying people for a change!"

For some reason, even though we sat there watching them, the monkeys ignored us until one huge alpha male came and sat next to us. Surprisingly, he didn't threaten or bully us despite the fact that we were carrying a packet of fruits. He just directed his troops towards other targets, occasionally ran out to personally lead them, and returned to his seat next to us.

After a while, Sam got nervous and decided that he had enough, "I think it's time we move. You do know that Rhesus Macaques carry diseases that have no cure."

"Relax! We are following in the footsteps of Lord Hanuman himself. He won't let anything bad happen to us!" Sri exclaimed.

"I'm not sure if your monkey friend next to us got the Lord's memo especially considering how he keeps staring me down," Sam countered.

"I find your lack of faith disturbing."

"I find it ironic that you used a Darth Vader quote to show your conviction in God," I exclaimed.

"We do what we must because we can," was his reply.

We shared some fruits with the alpha in a friendly, non-threatening manner and left. I was surprised how the monkey, which was such a bully to others, was so friendly towards us. Maybe, just maybe, the Lord was truly watching over us! Things like these are what make you want to *believe*. Sure, they could just be coincidences, but they certainly inspire faith.

We eventually checked into a hotel at Dabaspet to end a long and eventful day. I was desperate to get some decent shuteye, but it just wasn't meant to be. We were awakened at around midnight, by some furious banging on our door. I opened the door with a knife in my hand only to find a police officer there. Luckily, I managed to hide the knife behind my back before he noticed it. Apparently, the police had raided the lodge and were checking all the rooms for any illegal activities. He asked me if I had '*company*' and without waiting for a reply, glanced into the room to check. Talk about a lack of faith. Once he was satisfied that there was nothing illegal going on under his noble watch, he left with a disappointed look on his face.

As I closed the door and lay on the bed, I wondered where this journey was leading me. After the dream and the initial few *"signs"* (if they were even signs), there wasn't much that had affected my faith or my journey. It was just the usual walking, talking, and counting distances and places. Where was this going, I wondered. Was there anything I was going to accomplish though this? I didn't even know what I was looking for. Was it an experience? Another dream? Maybe some wisdom? Finally, I got tired of thinking about it and convinced myself that tomorrow was another day and that it would bring in something definitive.

Day 8: Master Splinter doesn't approve

Location: Dabaspet, Karnataka

The last temple we planned to visit before reaching Bengaluru was the Yoga Lakshmi Narasimha temple, located in the Devarayanadurga forest range. After walking through dry scrublands for the last few days, travelling through forest cover was a nice change. Upon arriving at the Yoga Narasimha Temple, we found the priests chasing two huge bandicoots around the inner sanctum. After thirty minutes, of leading the priests on a merry chase and playing a lot of hide and seek, the coots were finally killed.

Considering that, they were worshipped in the Karni Mata Temple, hunting them down and killing them seemed pretty damn ironic. If the rodents could understand our language, the conversation would have probably been something on these lines, "Hey you, yes you bandicoots. We don't serve your kind here. I mean seriously, what sort of establishment do you think this is? We only serve sanctioned animals here. You need to go to the Karni Mata Temple in Deshnoke. Oh, and on your way out, send the lions in."

Nevertheless, the priests at the temple were friendly and courteous towards us and treated us with kindness despite our looking far more scraggly than the bandicoots. While we felt bad about the killing of the bandicoots, it was still heart-warming to know that there were places where people did not judge or treat you differently based on appearance. Funny how humanity was capable of both the greatest deeds of good and acts of pure evil.

After visiting the temple, we went to see the *Namada Chilume*, a natural spring. Legend has it that Lord Rama, while wandering around these jungles during his exile, couldn't find water to apply *namam* on his forehead. So he shot an arrow into the ground and used the water that sprung out to smear *namam* on his forehead (hence the name of the place). The water flows to this day and is supposed to never dry up, even in summer. There was a small deer park nearby and plenty of monkeys there as well. While we sat at the park, Sri decided he was hungry, pulled out a packet of chips, and started munching away.

"You do know that that stuff will kill you," Sam said, matter-of-factly.

"I'm eating it to protect myself from the vampires," Sri retorted.

"Huh...what? Does he always act this weird?" Sam asked me.

"Trust me. Do you know why vampires always look good? It's because they are very health conscious. You know – five small meals a day, only organic blood, workouts, avoid Vitamin D. So yeah, if I eat junk, I will be unhealthy food for them and they will keep away," was Sri's response.

"Eat shit and die. If you don't want good advice, just say so."

"Ha ha ha…Enough fooling around minions. Let's get to Bengaluru and chill out," I said.

We took an auto-rickshaw back to Dabaspet and started walking towards Bengaluru. My feet were in good shape and there were no blisters or cramps, which was a good sign. The pack weighed heavily on my shoulders though and I realised that I had to get rid of the excess weight before we headed into the hill sections of the trek.

For the most part, we stuck close to the National Highway on the walk from Dabaspet to Bengaluru. Since there were no trees, vegetation, or any sort of shelter along the highway, it turned out to be very long and tiring. The sun beat down on us mercilessly and completely destroyed us. We had done several treks before, but none of them could prepare us for this. We were used to trekking in thick forest cover and places where the sun didn't shine as brightly. This definitely wasn't one of them.

The fact that I was supremely unfit did little to help me either. A year earlier, I was on the opposite end of the struggle. I was practicing martial arts like a maniac, where a typical session consisted of an hour of cardio, around a thousand kicks and punches, and an assortment of other punishment – all of that, twice a day. I was freakishly fit, but it all went kaput when I suffered a fracture. It was around this time that my grandma passed away. I should have gone back to my workouts once my injury healed; the hard work and discipline would have helped me deal with the situation better, but I didn't. Instead, I did the stupidest thing possible; I gave up on everything and took up the one fix solution to all of life's problems – alcohol.

For three months after my grandma's death, all I did was go to work, come back home and drink myself to sleep. Did it solve any of my problems? No. Then why did I do it? Simply because it helped me numb out the pain of losing her. If I couldn't remember it, it couldn't hurt me. Right? Eventually, I skipped the working part and went directly to the drinking part. In my alcohol-induced haze, I blamed God for everything that was wrong with me and around me. I concluded that such an unjust and merciless god didn't deserve to be worshipped. I stopped believing, gave up on prayer, and completely lost my faith in everything and everybody.

I thought things couldn't get any worse, but they did. I had an accident, thanks in no small part because I was driving, while being completely plastered. The result was a concussion plus wounds and bruises all over my body. It could have been worse, if not for the helmet and all the protective gear I was wearing, but I didn't realise it. I was so far gone that the first thing I did once I was back home was have another drink. I didn't care about anything anymore.

It was at this point that I had the dream for the first time. The dream sobered me up and made me think about what was happening. It gave me hope, raised me from that pit of misery I was wallowing in, and brought me to where I was now. All I had to do now was buck up, keep walking, and wonder WHY THE HELL IT WASN'T RAINING IN THE MONSOON SEASON!

We took plenty of breaks thanks to the heat, but every break only resulted in Sri and Sam getting into intense arguments. They kept arguing over stupid things until they finally realised that the energy was better spent on the walk and shut up. We kept drinking plenty of water, but it seemed to flow out as soon as we took a sip and we remained perpetually thirsty. The one thing that kept us going on was the fact that every step that we took brought us closer to some much-needed R&R.

Eventually, after a lot of walking and complaining, we managed to reach the outskirts of Bengaluru and caught a bus to our friend's (let's call him "*Bear*") place.

PART – 2: Humility

"We come nearest to the great when we are great in humility."

— Rabindranath Tagore

Days 9 to 11: Hulk smash puny kitten

Location: Bengaluru, Karnataka

In Bengaluru, as we recuperated, I was forced to reconsider my argument about the weight of my backpack. Over the past few days, my pack had weighed so heavily on my back that I readily surrendered myself to Sam and Sri for indoctrination into the cult 'Ultralight'. My training commenced with me being forced to throw out the water filter and packets of food, all while chanting, "His name is *Katadyn* water filter...his name is rice flakes....his name is condensed milk..." Since we hadn't faced any problems in terms of availability of food and water until then, I wasn't too worried about losing the water filter and the extra food. The zealots then proclaimed that my backpack was "too heavy" and forced me to buy a new 40 Litre *Wildcraft* backpack. Anything that they didn't feel comfortable with, was thrown out ruthlessly. At the end of my initiation, my backpack was lighter by at least five Kgs and I felt a lot more confident for the journey ahead.

We revisited the route for the next leg and since we hadn't found any contrary information, decided to continue with our initial assumption that *Lanka* was Sri Lanka. Sri suggested a quick detour to visit Mysore and Brahmagiri, so after a couple of days of rest, we went to visit the Rama Sita temple in Ramnagaram. According to legend, Lord Rama, Sita Devi, and Lakshman visited this temple together, and the temple was fairly well known for this reason. Then in the 70s, Bollywood came to Ramnagaram and shot a film called '*Sholay*'. The film's astronomical success ensured that it completely overshadowed the mythological legacy of the temple and side lined it. We entered the temple, quickly said our prayers, and headed to Mysore. Once there, we visited the Brindavan Gardens and the KRS Dam.

"I swear I'm going to kill myself if this trip will be as boring as it was today. Honestly, I have no clue why we are visiting places like this. An absolute waste of a day," Sam said, out of the blue.

Sri felt the need to defend his choice of places to visit, "The gardens are supposed to look beautiful with all the lights and the fountains at night."

"The only way this place can look beautiful is if someone burnt it to the ground. Imagine millions of bright embers floating into the black night, the slow shift from dark to light, and the leaves turning from green to black and then to nothing."

"Talk about being a jerk. Why don't you go and..."

"Can't a guy make a joke about setting things on fire without being burnt at the stake for it? Black humour is dead. Long live black humour."

"I have nothing to say to a moron," Sri replied.

"Aww, extra chromosome getting you *down*?"

"Lay off him," I said, trying to nip the fight in the bud.

"I pity the fool who is actually bothered about what a moron says," Sam said in his snarkiest tone and the argument began afresh.

Another wonderful day, where I had to stop my trip from disintegrating. I wondered if it would have been easier if I did the trip alone instead of carrying this baggage. Whatever be the case, I still had to stop them from tearing out each other's throats.

"Sri, you have to admit, this wasn't the best of days. Let's just leave it at that," I said, in an attempt to contain the damage.

"No more lawns and gardens. You guys are making me lazy. Every day that is spent not getting stronger, smarter, or faster is a day wasted and I seem to have plenty of such days, thanks to your stupid planning," Sam said.

All of a sudden, Sri started chanting, "Remember the black kitten. Remember the black kitten..."

"What the hell are you rambling about?" I asked.

"It's a long story."

"We have all the time in the world."

"So I had this dream..."

Sam cut in, "What's with both of you? Is that all you do? Dream?"

Sri ignored him and continued his story, "In the dream, I was extremely angry at someone and was shouting at them over the phone. A black kitten walked over and started scratching my foot. I shooed it away initially, but it kept coming back and eventually pissed on my leg. By that time, I was furious and kicked it away. I had never experienced such raw anger ever in my life. The kitten ran back at me and bit my leg."

"What happened after that?"

"I picked it up, throttled it, and pulled at its head. It started wailing, and I realised that I was hurting it and put it down. I looked at my hand and noticed that I had somehow pulled its face off; the kitten was walking around with no face, only a pink fleshy head. I was horrified and tried putting its face back on, but it didn't work, so to put it out of its misery I decided to strangle and kill it."

"And then?"

"I woke up, drenched in sweat, and in tears at the depravity of my act. The dream felt so real that I couldn't stop thinking about it. Eventually after a lot of deliberation, I arrived at a conclusion. For a few weeks before I had the dream, I had been angry about several things and had kept it bottled up inside of me. Obviously, it hadn't done me any good and had only served to make me angrier. The dream was a divine lesson - to point out the evils of anger and the futility of holding on to it."

"So you are not going to get angry from now on. That's nice," Sam said with a mischievous gleam in his eyes.

"I'm working hard at it. Every time I get angry, I remind myself of the kitten."

"I'm so happy that you told us your dream. From now on, we can take your case and all you can do is grit your teeth and say 'black kitten'."

"The dream was so sick and messed up that my heart is racing even now as I am telling you the story. I feel like a psychopath for even having that dream," Sri continued.

"Everybody is a psychopath. It's just a matter of perspective. From a mosquito's point of view, all humans are psychopaths. Think about it. A mosquito is flying around, just doing its thing. Suddenly it feels hungry, thinks 'I gotta get some food' and sees dinner. It says 'Thank you dear God, for our daily blood' and settles down to eat. Suddenly, **wham.** Dead. 'WTF? You psychopath! I was just having my dinner'," I said, trying to be supportive.

"Remind me to never sleep anywhere close to him. I shall now pray to God and thank him for giving me the two sanest travel buddies a guy could ever wish for!" Sam exclaimed.

We headed to a hotel in Mysore and I settled down with '*Childhood's End*', by Arthur C Clarke and hoped there wouldn't be any raiding that night.

Day 12: First we kill the hobbites, next we take the Precious, and then...we sell it on Amazon

Location: Mysore, Karnataka

The next morning as I was brushing my teeth, I noticed that my ears were completely sunburned, to the point that the skin had started peeling off and were sensitive to the touch. Guess that was the reason why they applied sunblock to every orifice possible in the ads. Nothing much to do about it so I pushed my ears into my cap and we headed out to see Mysore.

We visited the Chamundi temple – a *Maha Shakti Peetha* dedicated to the Goddess Chamundi (the principal deity of Mysore) in the morning and the Mysore palace in the evening. The palace was the residence of the rulers of Mysore, the Wodeyars and additionally served as a museum of sorts. We took a tour of the museum and stayed back until it got dark, to see the display of the palace with all of its lights on. It was truly magnificent and was something that all of us including Sam enjoyed.

After the sightseeing tour, we went to a restaurant to have dinner and ordered some rotis, dal, palak, and curd rice. The food arrived and Sri promptly blew his top.

"What the hell! Why does the curd rice have pomegranates, grapes, and carrots in it? What manner of devious plot is this? Who in his right mind would ever commit such sacrilege?"

"I thought that was quite common in the south. I have seen pomegranates in curd rice a lot of times myself," Sam said.

"That is a cardinal sin of gastronomy. That's as bad as say, making sweet *sambar* or sugar omelettes, or heaven forbid vegetarian *haleem*. The ones who commit these sins will be sent to hell and forced to eat *karela* cake for the rest of eternity."

"I think you better start chanting now…black kitten, black

kitten. At least we can convince people than you are insane and ask for a discount."

I couldn't blame Sri though, the guy loved his food. He was perpetually hungry and munching on something or the other, be it extremely healthy food or flat out junk. The only thing I ever saw him get worked up over was food or the lack of it. All you had to do to keep him happy was feed him – sort of like a puppy, which made him far easier to deal with compared to Sam.

Day 13: I may be bad, but I feel good...

Location: Mysore, Karnataka

After a tedious three-hour journey from Mysore involving multiple bus transfers, we ended up at Sri Mangalam. The plan was to meet the Range officer and get permits to visit Brahmagiri, Irupu falls, and the Munikal cave (according to legend, this was the cave that Lord Rama, Lakshman, and Hanuman stumbled upon in their search for Sita Devi). However, that wasn't to be; it rained so heavily that day that even the trees on the Brahmagiri range probably felt miserable.

All we could manage was a visit to the Irupu Ramasamy temple, which according to legend was where Lord Lakshman shot an arrow into the ground and caused a river to spring up – hence the name, Lakshmana Teertha. I wanted to stay back and visit the Munikal cave, but the *tyranny of majority* was brought into play and we headed back to town to find a nice homestay and enjoy some of the Coorgi Pork.

As I lay in the warm, comfortable bed of the homestay, I again wondered where this journey was heading. Two weeks in and I still wasn't any closer to any answers that would help my faith. Doubt and regret still weighed heavily on my mind. I realised that all the while that I was walking, none of these thoughts would occur to me. It was only at night did I have these overwhelming thoughts of regret and doubt. The idle mind truly was the devil's workshop.

After tossing and turning in my bed for a few hours, worrying about the purpose of this journey, I realised that there was nothing I could really do except ignore the doubts and continue onward. Ignoring them was easier said than done though. Every time I ignored them, they came back stronger than before; they brought in new questions and insecurities and opened up old wounds to torment me. It was only a matter of time before they would come back with enough strength to break through whatever little faith and willpower I had and overwhelm me. Time was running out and I was getting desperate.

"It is the nature of doubt to use your greatest dream to destroy you. The bigger the dream, the easier its destruction, and yours, since bigger dreams have more gremlins to work with."

Day 14: An Inconvenient Truth

Location: Somewhere near Madikeri, Karnataka

Upon waking up, we received some bad news. The previous day's rain was not a local one-off occurrence; the monsoon was coming in fast and we only had a brief window of opportunity before all trekking routes in and around Male Mahadeshwara (MM) hills were closed off. If we missed it, we would have to wait for several months before the route would be open again. We debated on whether we could take a chance with the monsoon and walk to MM hills, but considering how heavily it had rained the previous day, it would have been a huge gamble. We made a judgment call and hopped onto a bus heading towards MM hills.

The views became increasingly picturesque as we approached MM hills. All around us, we could see the huge peaks (there are around 77 hills in this forest range) and deep valleys of the Satyamangala range. The range is renowned for its huge variety of plants and animals, especially elephants and was where the notorious smuggler Veerappan used to operate. After his death, the forest department had reopened several trails in the area and we planned to follow one of them to the Tamil Nadu border.

After getting to MM hills, we tried to get a room at the Temple guesthouse, but were informed by the authorities that the room would not be given out to '*singles*' (yeah, that was the exact word used) without the permission of the local police. They also told us that we '*singles*' could get a room in a nearby private lodge at the same price. My ego rose to the occasion and I worked myself into a rage, "*How could they refuse to let us stay here? It's a temple guesthouse! They don't own it and they can't turn away perfectly decent people, especially someone who is on the Lord's trip. I was the one who had the dream, not these fat pigs. Who were they to judge me? I would stay at* **this** *very guesthouse and show them."*

Sri tried to calm me down but to no avail, so off we went to the police station. The head constable patiently heard of the grave injustice meted out to us before finally saying, "Fine! Go back to the temple and tell them that the police is OK with you staying in the temple guesthouse."

Armed with the words of power, we went back to the temple guesthouse and told them that the police said it was fine. However, the officials at the guesthouse once again refused, and said they needed the police permit as indemnity. (As if a handwritten piece of paper would keep me in check if I turned out to be a homicidal maniac!) So back to the police station we went, where this gem of a conversation took place:

"The authorities at the guesthouse insisted on a written slip. Could you please give me the slip?" I asked.

"You do not need it," the cop replied.

"Well, they insisted."

"Ok. Show me some ID proof."

"Here is my passport and my driver's license."

The cop looked closely at the license and passport and then said, "But I do not know you."

"What do you think ID cards are for, you dimwit?" I muttered under my breath.

"I'm going to kick this guy on the head. I'm sure it will make him smarter," Sam whispered to us.

"Do you have to kick everyone?" Sri asked.

"The next time a cop wants to see my license, I will ask him to produce his grandmother as proof that he is a cop."

We argued with him for thirty minutes before he gave up, saying that he would refer our case to his supervisor, and asked us to come back after an hour. We decided to use the time to get the trekking permits and return to the police station after that. In stark contrast to the police constable and the authorities at the guesthouse, the forest officer was very understanding and after approving the trek, offered us accommodation at the forest department's guesthouse.

This simple act of kindness calmed my mind and brought back rational thought. It was only then that I realised how egotistical I was being. I felt that I deserved better treatment, as I was walking along the *Hanuman route* (as if that gave us special privileges). My behaviour stood in stark contrast to one of the key ideals that Lord Hanuman stood for – humility. I felt ashamed and realised that I had to change for the better, if I ever hoped to get my faith back. I immediately gave up my ego trip and took up the forest officer's offer thus ending our quest for a place to stay.

After a quick shower, we visited the Male Mahadeshwara temple, an ancient temple dedicated to Lord Shiva in the *form* of Sri Mahadeshwara. There was a huge crowd gathered at the entrance of the temple, as it was an auspicious day and there was a ceremonial procession, taking place. The priest at the temple told us that the temple was over five hundred years old and explained the legend associated with it. He also informed us that the temple was famous for its *Anna Daan*, where thousands of devotees were offered free food every day.

Later that evening, as we sat down for dinner, my new best friend – doubt, turned up once again. He had come up with a new angle, *"Aren't you supposed to be walking the entire way? How would Lord Hanuman feel about your little bus ride? That's clearly a shortcut, which means you fucked up. Why do you think you haven't seen any 'signs' lately, huh?"*

He was trying to break me down by putting a genuinely terrifying thought into my head – the thought that I wasn't being *true* to my dream; that the only way I could get my faith was to go back and walk the whole way. He clearly knew that even suggesting that we take a single step back at this point, would start a fight among the three of us, and make us think about ending the journey (not that I didn't do that on an hourly basis).

Since we were in this together for better or worse, I decided to be honest and share my doubts with Sam and Sri. Sam said that the *sanctity* of the journey had indeed been compromised, but only because there hadn't been any practical alternative. If we hadn't caught a bus to shorten this specific part of our journey, we would likely have been stuck for the entire rainy season when the monsoons hit. Then we wouldn't have had to worry about maintaining the *sanctity* of the journey, simple because there wouldn't have been any journey! That was how he justified our lapse or at least how he viewed it.

Sri, on the other hand, immediately understood what was on my mind. (It probably helped that he had higher emotional perception than a brain dead zombie, unlike the other fool.) He asked me not to think about it too much and said that every trip had its highs and lows and since in my case, I was virtually venturing into the unknown, the lows would be well, low. My purpose, the route we were following, and my destination were all unclear, he pointed out. Doubt was inevitable when there were so many unknowns and he thought I should have known this when we started our journey. Whatever be the case, we were like the explorers of old, he said. The ones who overcame their doubts succeeded and those who could not, failed. It all depended on how well I could deal with my doubts.

I realised that his words made complete sense. It was completely normal to have doubts. Only a mad man wouldn't have doubts, when faced with so many unknowns. However, the only solution I could come up with was to keep plugging the doubts and hoping the dam would hold, until I found some real answers. Considering how strong my doubt had become, I knew that I had very little time before I would crash and burn.

Day 15: Killing is as easy as breathing

Location: MM hills, Karnataka

I woke up feeling fresh and firmly resolved to push doubt to the back of my mind and just focus on the trek. We met the forest officer, who once again went out of his way to find someone, who would guide us through the forests. We wished all forest officials were as helpful, trekkers would be far better off.

The trek was supposed to be a two-day affair – day one to cover the fourteen kilometres to Nagamale and day two to cover the remaining eight kilometres to Palar check post on the Tamil Nadu border. Since it was completely overcast that morning, we had a quick discussion with our guide and decided to do the trek in a single day; a difficult task but certainly not an impossible one.

We started at 9 a.m., and followed a trail that wound around several hills and passed through deep valleys. In order to have any chance of completing the trek in one day, we attacked the trail at a pace that could almost be called 'jogging'. The initial stretch of the trek had several steep ascents and descents that we struggled to get past, especially since the sun was shining brightly down on us. (How the weather changed from 'Walking in wet underwear isn't fun' to 'Time to make omelettes' in just a couple of hours was beyond me.) Nevertheless, after a few hours of walking we reached Nagamale village.

A short break later, we went to visit the Nagamale temple, which is located about a kilometre from the village. As it was a temple path, we chose to walk along it without any footwear. The path was full off uneven rocks with sharp edges and they were super-hot thanks to the blazing sun. Walking on these rocks ensured that my feet were completely blistered and to make matters worse, I stepped on a particularly sharp rock and ended up with a deep cut on my foot.

At Nagamale temple, there are two rocks, one of which resembles a *Linga* and the other resembles a large three-headed snake (*Naga*). The *snake rock* is positioned in such a way that it appears as if it is protecting the *Linga*, hence the name *Nagamale*. The view of the Cauvery and the surrounding peaks from the top of Nagamale was fantastic and we took a bunch of photos before heading back.

After returning to the village, we had a quick lunch, put our shoes back on, and started down the trail towards Palar. Since the trail was very steep and rocky, my blistered feet started to hurt. I tried taping them up, but to no avail, they insisted on traumatizing me. The cut on my foot started chafing against my shoe and I tried putting some cotton to reduce the friction. It wasn't of much help because after every few steps, the cotton kept flying out. Since there was nothing else I could do about it, I braced myself and continued walking. It was painful, but I could be stubborn at times and refused to show any weakness in front of the others, something that I had in common with Sam.

Eventually, we reached Palar check post at 6 p.m., thoroughly exhausted and desperate for a nice shower and a comfortable bed. However, that wasn't meant to be since there were no amenities available there – no shelter, no electricity, no food, nothing. We hitched a ride in a truck to a nearby village, had dinner, and returned to the check post after which the guide went on his way. Since there was no accommodation, we settled down to sleep along with the forest guards, next to a small temple near the check post. My back and shoulders hurt, but I was more concerned about my feet. I applied some medication to them and hoped that the wounds would heal quickly, as we still had plenty of walking ahead of us.

While Sri slept soundly, Sam and I hardly got any sleep, thanks to his misanthropy and my paranoia. Sleeping here in the open, near strangers, I felt exposed. I had slept in forests several times with nary a worry. Here amidst people though, I couldn't sleep peacefully because I expected the worst from them. As I lay awake, listening to their snores, I realised that I had a long way to go in terms of having faith in my fellow human beings. After a couple of hours, I drifted into sleep due to sheer exhaustion.

In the middle of the night, a lorry squealed to a halt at the check post and in an instant, I was up with a knife in my hand. The forest guards, who were sleeping close by also woke up and freaked out looking at the knife in my hand. They must have thought I was a lunatic, because the next day when we woke up, we found them sleeping on the other side of the temple, as far away from me as possible. As you sow, so shall you reap, in this case it was distrust. I guess I couldn't expect others to trust me, when I was so distrustful myself.

On the bright side, my paranoia ensured that there was no opportunity for doubt to creep back in. My worry about being stabbed in my sleep, by some random stranger, was greater than my worry about the purpose of my journey. Apparently, the easiest way to get rid of something you are worried about is to mess up in a bigger way and worry about that. Considering our track record that wouldn't be too hard a task.

Day 16: Ten thousand thundering typhoons!

Location: Palar check post, border of Karnataka and Tamil Nadu

I woke up the next morning and felt much better despite my disturbed sleep. My foot still hurt from the cut, but since the distance to Mettur was only around twenty-five kilometres, I figured it wouldn't be a problem. The forest guards found it amusing that we weren't hitching a ride to Mettur. By then, they had probably decided that we were psychotic, so they just waved us off and told us to watch out for the monkeys and crocodiles. After an hour of walking, we ran across a monkey, which had lost one of its limbs. Feeling pity for it, I decided to give it a banana.

"NOOOOOO! Don't!" Sam screamed.

"What is wrong with you? Can't you see the poor thing has an arm missing?" Sri asked.

"Haven't you guys ever seen boards saying 'Don't feed the monkeys'? Do you remember what the forest guards said?"

I ignored Sam and gave the banana to the monkey. He could be an asshole at times. It was obvious that the poor thing was hungry and meant us no harm.

"Oh man. You had to do that right?"_

He was now getting on my nerves, "Come on. What can go wrong with feeding a poor monkey?"

"I'm sure the thirty odd monkeys sitting behind you agree wholeheartedly. Now, please start the banana distribution. I assume you have thirty bananas right?"

"Oh Shit...Ok new plan. I throw this banana in that direction and we run in the opposite direction as fast as possible," I said.

"This is the reason why I say the world would be a better place if people listened to me. That's all you have to do. Listen to me!"

"I recommend less talking and more running unless you think you can convince the monkeys to listen to you."

Thanks to the running, we worked up quite an appetite and at the next village proceeded to have a solid breakfast of dosas with chicken and eggs at a breakfast shack. After breakfast, we resumed walking and faced a problem we hadn't anticipated and it was quite a serious one; one with teeth – dogs! The mongrels were everywhere. They snarled at us menacingly and chased us around. Over a three-kilometre stretch, we were threatened by seven dogs and we realised there was no going forward without either getting bitten or figuring out why they were specifically picking on us even in a large group of people. Was it what we were wearing, what we were carrying, or the way we looked? We tried several experiments before eventually discovering what was pissing them off.

Experiment 1: With cap on – Woof Woof.

Experiment 2: Without cap on – Met with tail wagging.

Experiment 3: Remove and put on cap alternatively – Woof Woof and attacked us!

So there we were, walking along and doffing our caps to every mongrel in sight in every village. It was no wonder that many villagers found this extremely amusing. After passing a particularly *doggy village,* Sri stopped to buy a pack of biscuits for a starving dog, which had its ribs showing. Maybe he hoped our doggy *karma* would improve with this. Surprisingly, it did. The villages from there on had very few dogs and they weren't aggressive either. They just left us alone for some reason. Good karma for the win, I guess. Once we hit the main road, it wasn't a difficult walk, but the cut on my foot started bleeding and showed signs of infection. I had taken some antibiotics, but they didn't seem to be helping.

Earlier the monkeys and the mongrels had distracted me from the pain, but after they left us alone, I had nothing better to think about and the pain returned with a vengeance. Every step hurt and I tried everything, including adjusting my walking style, but to no avail. Eventually, I surrendered myself to the pain and walked the last few kilometres into Mettur with it. I hoped to make it to the end of the leg in Coimbatore, where a few days of rest would let it heal.

Day 17: Hell Week

Location: Mettur, Tamil Nadu

It was one of those days, the ones in which you have huge ups and downs. Like tornados, they come rarely, but when they do, they toss you all over the place, cause major devastation, and leave you wondering about what the hell happened and what you would do next. The day started well enough; we woke up quite late and were well rested. My foot seemed to be okay, but just to be on the safe side, I taped some cotton between the cut and my socks to prevent any chafing. We had breakfast and started walking on a path next to the Cauvery River. It was a pleasant walk with plenty to see – riverine vistas, flora and fauna, and people going about their daily business.

We walked slowly taking in the sights and after a few hours had covered a distance of eleven kilometres. After this divine stretch, we were forced back onto the National Highway, thanks to two reasons – private property and the four-legged demons that we dare not speak of. Apparently, doggy karma only lasted for a day. At one point even a goat got into the act, it was a particularly nasty one and charged at us. Luckily, for us it was tied up and ran out of rope before we got the horn up our nether regions.

As we walked, my foot started to hurt and the pain grew worse with every step. The swelling that formed around the cut seemed to indicate that it was infected. I continued walking, while trying to shut out the pain as much as I could by focusing on the river. The fact that the sun had come up and was now burning down on us didn't help us one bit. Whoever said walking was therapeutic should be whipped and staked through the heart.

We were around twenty kilometres from Mettur, when the river separated from the road and we slowly lost sight of it.

The cut on my foot started bleeding and no matter how much I tried, I couldn't patch it up. Every step hurt and at one point out of sheer desperation, I took off my shoes and tried to walk in my socks for some relief from the pain. It didn't help, except to serve as a harsh reminder that I still had blistered feet. The river had been peaceful and calming and the cool breeze kept me in high spirits. Once I lost sight of it, I seemed to lose all my energy. I had no motivation left to move forward – no beautiful sight at the next turn of the river, no breeze dancing around me keeping me cool, and nothing to remind me that there was something good coming up.

The doubt lingering in my mind finally found the opening he was looking for and rushed in to take up the opportunity, *"Let me ask you something. Don't you think this whole idea is stupid? Wouldn't it be better to sit at home or in a temple and pray? I mean, that's what everybody else who found peace or nirvana, or anything meaningful did. They sat and meditated.*

How is this walk helping? What do you think you will get by walking a thousand kilometres? Nothing. NOTHING. Think about it. You haven't gotten any real signs since you started, they were all just a bunch of coincidences. If God was really watching, you should have gotten a sign by now. You misinterpreted a dream and took it too far. It's ok, it happens; we all make mistakes. Now let's go back home. There's nothing left to be done here."

For an hour, I trudged along battling the doubt in my head. However, with the sun burning down and my foot hurting like hell, doubt cemented his place in my head. I questioned why I was doing this in the first place and why I shouldn't just go to a temple and pray if I wanted my faith back. All the negativity and disbelief inside me poured out and I thought that it was incredibly stupid to be walking along a National Highway in the blazing sun, when I could have been at home, relaxing. This wasn't how I imagined it would be; we would be walking in cloudy weather with a cool breeze guiding us, joking and laughing our way to each of our destinations. In reality, I was limping along a hot and dusty National Highway with a foot that could probably be amputated in a couple of days. This was bullshit; I wasn't going to do this anymore.

It was at this point that the dam broke and I lost all motivation to continue walking. I gave up on the journey, sat down under a tree next to the road, and refused to move. No matter what my buddies said to motivate me, I couldn't push forward. I asked the guys to go ahead without me, but they were unwilling to do so. So we all sat silently under the tree, until Sri convinced me to talk to my dad and seek his advice. I called my dad and explained the situation.

"I think I'm done here. I had enough and am coming home," I said. "This is just stupid. Why the hell am I running this fool's errand? Why didn't you stop me in the first place and tell me this was a stupid idea?"

My dad listened patiently as I vented and asked me, "Why are you doing this trip?"

"You know the dream right?"

"I don't need an explanation. I'm just reminding you of your reason for doing this and why it's important to you."

"It's hot here, I'm dehydrated, my feet are torn open, and I have no energy or motivation."

"You are always welcome back, but you do realise that you are going to torture yourself over this. Right?"

The old man was right. I would definitely struggle with it for the rest of my life, if I didn't finish what I had started. My dad must have sensed that I was in two minds and needed some motivation, so he decided to do what he did best – give me a lecture.

"Did you know that US Navy SEALS go through a week of training called *Hell Week,* which is a hundred plus hours of continuous physical exertion with almost no sleep or rest?" he asked. "It's physically impossible. Yet, every year the strongest of the SEALS get through this. How do you think they do it? The physical body has limitations, but the mind only has those that you impose on it yourself."

"Have you been reading, *The Secret*?" I asked sarcastically.

"No, but I have read, *How to make excuses and pussyfoot around*. Do you want me to mail you a copy?"

"Okay…fine, I get it. I will man up and finish what I started, but I'm a little concerned about the foot. It's bleeding and the swelling seems to indicate infection."

"There is a thin line between being tough and being stupid. Just take a bus to the nearest town, get your foot looked at, and then take a call."

Since what my dad suggested seemed logical, we decided to catch a bus to Bhavani. We had to walk two kilometres to reach a bus stop, where we could catch the bus though, oh the sweet sweet irony! After reaching Bhavani, Sri suggested that we visit the Arulmigu Hanumantharaya Swamy temple in Gobichettipalayam, as we had some time to kill. Since it wasn't too far away and since I was feeling better after the rest, we headed to the temple and upon arriving, found it to be closed. It was supposed to open in an hour so we decided to wait.

It was at that moment that I had one of the most amazing experiences of the trip. As we were sitting outside the temple, I started reading the *Hanuman Chalisa* and at one point of time *zoned* out completely. It's hard to explain the feeling, for one fleeting moment my mind was completely clear and I didn't have any worries, pains, fears, or even thoughts – not my feet, not my bag and shoes being stolen (they were outside and I was worried about them until then), not money, nothing at all. Then it was gone.

This was what I was looking for – a moment of peace, something I hadn't had in a long time and what I desperately craved. It brought back feelings and memories, good ones, from a time long past. I had meditated earlier and experienced the feeling of having an empty mind with no thoughts. That feeling wasn't even close to this in terms of how peaceful and happy I felt. I was unsure of what it was and whether it was related to my reading the *Chalisa* or just a creation of an exhausted mind, but it was there and I was curious.

I was describing the experience to Sri and Sam, when the priest arrived and opened the temple doors. We went in, offered our prayers, and talked to the priest. Even with the language barrier, he managed to provide us with a wealth of information on the route, places and temples to visit. He also showed us an old map of the region that contained details of the various Hanuman temples. He seemed to agree on the route we were taking, but then nobody had any definite proof or evidence on the same; it was only speculation.

My dad called to check on me, but he needn't have worried. I had already made up my mind on what I was going to do. The experience in the temple had brought back my motivation. I had read about things related to *Nirvana, Kundalini energy,* unlocking *Chakra-gates,* and other such phenomenon, but hadn't practically experienced those concepts before this incident. The fact that I experienced it when I needed it the most made me assume that there was more to it than pure coincidence. The best case was that it was a *sign* and that it was in some way connected to the trip. The worst case was that it was just a quirk of my mind. Both of these cases were interesting and warranted investigation and therein lay my motivation to go ahead and see where it led.

We headed to Namakkal (off route) to get my foot looked at and to visit the Namakkal Anjaneyar temple. For a change, we caught a bus and it was nice to see the kilometres pass by quickly. We take transportation for granted and only appreciate it when it isn't available; like so many other things in life.

Day 18: The good left undone

Location: Namakkal, Tamil Nadu

I was awakened early in the morning by a call from my father. For a guy who had done his share of travelling, he really got worked up over little things (ok, maybe not so little in this case, but still!). Thanks to his call, our first task for the day was to meet a doctor. The doctor took one look at my foot, figured it was infected, and gave me a Tetanus shot and some antibiotics that were strong enough to knock out a horse. Since I felt drowsy under the onslaught of the drugs, we decided to take it easy and visit the Namakkal Anjaneyar temple, which was located nearby.

At the first glance itself, we were awestruck. We had expected to see a typical statue of Lord Hanuman – small, disproportionate, and gaudily painted. What we saw instead was a huge statue, twenty feet tall, with a fierce warlike expression and a sword at his waist. This fifteen hundred plus year old statue had been painstakingly carved out of a single stone and was the best statue of Hanuman that we had ever seen. The statue is completely exposed to the elements and doesn't have a roof over it. The most remarkable aspect of the statue was the fact that despite being in the open for more than fifteen hundred years, it didn't look weathered in the least bit!

This was by far the best sight of the journey – a statue of Lord Hanuman, the warrior with a sword. The fact that we were completely surprised by the size and grandeur of the statue, only added to its beauty. We had a tendency of *Googling* everything as part of planning a trip and thus losing the excitement that came with experiencing a picturesque sight or a magnificent monument for the first time. The thrill of discovery was usually lost, so for this trip we decided not to look at any pictures of places that we planned to visit and it had paid off.

After a short while, we headed uphill to the Namakkal fort, which offered panoramic views of Namakkal. It was located close to the centre of Namakkal and once we got up there we could see the entire town.

"Look at all the people scurrying around like ants, rushing to work!" Sam exclaimed.

"And look at us with all the time in the world to sit, relax, and watch," I added.

"Sometimes it's good to slow down my friend. The only thing that could make it better is rubbing people's noses in it."

"Yeah, I'm sure you would know all about rubbing it in, don't you. I know about that particularly nasty hobby of yours, how you sit on the divider of a road on workdays during peak traffic and wave beer cans at the poor souls rushing to work," Sri said.

"Well, it's fun and I'm helping."

"It's fun for you, not for them! Besides, I'm not even sure how you could consider that as helping anyone? You are only making them feel miserable."

"I can't help it if people get jealous and stop being happy, just because some random bloke is merrily drinking beer on the road. Not my fault that it's human nature to be envious of what others have. It's a weakness and I just exploit it. The truly happy ones wave back at me with a smile on their faces, urging me to enjoy my day! Now, what does that tell you? People need to understand that I am not stopping them from being happy, they are stopping themselves from being happy!"

"The drones all slave away, they're working overtime,
They serve a faceless queen, they never question why.
Disciples of a God, that neither lives nor breathes,
But we have bills to pay, yeah we have mouths to feed!"
– Drones, Rise Against

After our visit to the fort, we caught a bus and headed to Coimbatore for some much needed rest.

PART – 3: Wisdom

"The only true wisdom is in knowing you know nothing."

— Socrates

Days 19 to 22: It's a magical world Hobbes ol' buddy. Let's go exploring!

Location: Coimbatore, Tamil Nadu

We spent a couple of days resting and catching up with old friends. Invariably, the conversation would always turn to my journey and the doubt I grappled with. Even though, all my friends had different opinions about my journey, they all seemed to agree on the reason why I was having so much doubt. Apparently, it stemmed from my deep-rooted obsession with details; details like - the distance covered (specifically walked), route taken, places visited etc. that were actually immaterial in the grand scheme of things. They recommended that I focus on the experience itself, rather than worrying about these details and reminded me of the following lines from Alice in Wonderland:

Alice: Would you tell me, please, which way I ought to go from here?

The Cheshire Cat: That depends a good deal on where you want to get to.

Alice: I don't much care where...

The Cheshire Cat: Then it doesn't much matter which way you go.

Alice: ...so long as I get somewhere.

The Cheshire Cat: Oh, you're sure to do that, if you only walk long enough.

I realized that they were right. This was in many ways, the trip of a lifetime. There were so many incredible things happening, so many sights to see, and people to meet, but instead I was counting kilometres and checking places to visit off my list. I had been a fool...! I decided to take it one day at a time, take in the sights, and just try to enjoy the walk. Sam and Sri also agreed and we vowed to focus more on doing what we all liked. We were far ahead of schedule anyway; we had planned to walk twenty kilometres per day but had been walking around thirty-forty kilometres per day. Besides, it was going to be the experience that would help my faith, not the walking itself.

We sat down and revisited our route for Leg three, to figure out how we could improve upon it. This involved more homework, more modifications to maps, and more debates. The biggest cause of disagreement regarding the route arose due to the 'Mysterious case of the disappearing Monkey God'. According to the Ramayana, Lord Hanuman and the monkey troop walked south for several weeks through numerous forests and searched many mountains in the *Vindhyas* (not to be confused with the present Vindhya Range) in their quest to find Lanka. Finally, struggling with fatigue and hunger, they stumbled upon a huge cave – the *Riksha bilam,* a magical cave abode created by Ravana's father-in-law, Maya. Upon entering the cave, they were offered shelter by the cave's caretaker, Swayamprabha. As the monkeys rested and recuperated inside the cave, Lord Hanuman told Swayamprabha about their quest to locate Lanka and their subsequent troubles. Moved by their plight, Swayamprabha ***sailed*** Lord Hanuman and the monkey troop directly to a peak near the shoreline, from where they could cross the sea and reach Lanka.

"What do they mean by ***sailed***? How did they get to the coastline? Did they walk there?" Sri asked.

"According to the Ramayana, it hardly took a minute for them to be ***sailed*** from somewhere in the middle of Tamil Nadu to the coast. Teleportation, perhaps?" I replied.

"Teleportation you say, eh laddie. I guess we are no longer *trekking,* but '*Startreking*'! Maybe we should try doing this trek after fifty years, when *Scotty's* beaming people around," Sam said.

"I think they actually walked all the way to the coast, or at least until the last mountain range. The cave just took them past the last mountain range. Remember, this was an army of fit monkeys, moving at incredible speeds. Walking twelve hundred kilometres in a month wouldn't be a big deal for them. Heck we are averaging close to thirty kilometres a day and we aren't even fit."

"Didn't the Ramayana also mention that there were *Vimanas* in the cave? You know, right? The ones that apparently flew by using principles of anti-gravity. Maybe they used one of those," Sri suggested.

"You know what I think? I think Big-Foot or the Yeti or perhaps even the Incredible Hulk carried the entire army to the seashore," Sam suggested.

"There is logical alternative to the teleportation theory. Every culture in the world has some reference to underground tunnels that connect the world. Similarly, there is a theory that there are a series of interconnected underground caves across South India. Think about it, most of the large temples in South India have underground tunnel entrances," Sri said, ignoring Sam.

"Something on the lines of *Agartha*?" I asked.

"Have either of you heard of Tin foil hats? Coz you sure as hell need them."

"Such a sceptic!"

"People tend to believe what matches their needs and desires, not what is logical or *kicking your ass – spitting in your face truth*!"

"Ironically, a lot of people also tend to believe a lot of bullshit as long as you say 'science', but to believe that God exists, everybody wants proof," Sri said, taking us down a path that nobody was keen on discussing, thus effectively ending the argument.

Since Sri insisted on visiting Kodaikanal, we decided to take a detour through Palani instead of going straight through to Dindigul. We tried to get permits from the forest officials to trek through the Palani Reserve Forest, but to no avail. As usual, the officials passed the buck and washed their hands off the issue. I called my dad and he asked us to look up the 1942 Forest Act to figure out the rules and regulations that would apply. The Forest Act only prohibited trapping and other activities like starting fires or damaging forest resources. Since it did not explicitly state anything against trekking/hiking, I figured that we were in the right and decided to go ahead. *Ignorantia juris non excusat*, be damned.

My dad also **informed** me that the family was coming down to Madurai to visit the Madurai and Rameshwaram temples with us. Since it was a statement, there was no questioning it. The old man's stubbornness could give donkeys a complex and I was no exception.

Thanks to the few days of rest we got at Coimbatore, the wounds on my feet had healed up and I was all set to walk again. In fact, I was raring to go, thanks to the series of pep talks that I got from my family and friends. Suddenly, everybody seemed to be excited with the idea of our finishing the journey, perhaps even more than us!

Day 23: Be like water

Location: Coimbatore, Tamil Nadu

Despite all the typical jackassery, we managed to get an early start from Coimbatore. We caught a bus to Mettur to the point where I had *quit* and started walking towards Bhavani. By 2 p.m., we were in Bhavani, where we made a quick visit to the Sangameswarar temple. Our next destination was Erode, and to get there we planned to follow a trail that ran along the Cauvery River. Somehow, we managed to miss the trail and get completely lost. There we were, thinking that it was impossible to get lost while using a GPS device, and yet we persisted and achieved it. *Impossible is nothing* – Adidas certainly would be proud! Eventually, we had to call home base and get step-by-step directions to the trail.

All of a sudden, Sam went ballistic, "At this rate we are never going to accomplish anything close to what Robert Scott, Amelia Earhart, or Roald Amundsen did."

"What exactly is that? Death under unknown circumstances?" I asked, in my snarkiest tone.

"I'm talking about being the first to accomplish something, dammit! The first to get to a place, see a sight, or accomplish something, something that nobody else has. It's the feeling of triumph and excitement that ..."

"So this is the reason why you agreed to do this trip without any questions," I said, interrupting him.

"Of course. It's the only reason I'm doing this trip with you guys. It's for the sense of achievement and the rush that you experience when you are doing it. It's pure unadulterated happiness."

"If that is the case then you wouldn't be still here considering that we blew the '*walking the entire Lord Hanuman route*' bit, long back. So what is actually keeping you here?"

"While we were in Coimbatore, planning the next stage of our journey, we joked about climbing Mount Mahendragiri. Well, guess what? I went online to read more about

Mahendragiri and I didn't find much about it; excluding a couple of research papers and books about the flora and fauna in that region, there is nothing about it especially about anyone climbing the mountain. I am not even sure if anyone has ever made it to the top. That is what's keeping me here, the prospect of a *first ascent*."

"Wow! You really are serious about climbing Mahendragiri! You saw the maps of the area; it looks very treacherous. Besides, it probably is a restricted area considering that ISRO has a facility near Mahendragiri. I'm not sure if there is any reason we should try climbing that mountain at all. It's too risky!" Sri said.

"Oh you want a reason? How about this? The *Valmiki Ramayana* references Mahendragiri as the mountain, which Lord Hanuman climbed, meditated on, and jumped off (to Lanka). There is also a legend, which says that there is an ancient *Vimana* complex located on Mahendragiri. So, I guess that's two reasons why we should climb Mahendragiri. Also, the ISRO complex isn't located anywhere close to Mahendragiri."

"Well if you put it that way, it makes some sense, but are we really prepared to climb that mountain? I am not sure if we have the right gear. The mountain seemed to be thickly forested, and when we checked the terrain on those maps, I could make out a few steep sections that probably are rocky cliffs. We should really think this through and not venture blindly into it," I said, trying to play the devil's advocate.

"Oh come on, you act as if it's Mt Everest that we are talking about. I think we have everything we need to climb a 5000ft mountain in a tropical forest," Sam said, dismissively.

"Seriously, Sam! Your obsession is borderline dangerous. Go easy, when making these 'all in or nothing' decisions. Seriously, do you even consider the risks? How much are you willing to risk for this?" Sri asked.

"Anything and everything. You guys wouldn't understand, but I feel truly alive only when I'm on the edge. What's the point of living if you don't experience that? Only when you come close to death do you truly understand and appreciate life. I would rather live for ten years and live life my way than just exist for fifty years doing nothing."

"What about your family and friends? Did you even consider how they would feel if anything happened to you?"

"We all have our lives to live. We came here alone and we will die alone. The day you understand that is the day you will truly be free."

"Please tell me you aren't planning on dying on this trip. I have enough to deal with as it is," I said.

"I'm not suicidal, so you don't have to worry about that. I have plenty of things to live for. "Anyway, Mahendragiri is near Nagercoil, while we are still in Coimbatore. We still have plenty of time ahead of us. Let's worry about it when we get to Nagercoil, that is, assuming our hero doesn't wimp out **again** before that," Sam said, in his usual sarcastic manner.

Once we were on the trail, walking along the river and later a rivulet was sheer joy. All along the way, we saw people diving in and enjoying the cool water. Eventually, after an hour of walking we couldn't resist any longer, stripped, and jumped in ourselves. Nothing could beat a swim in a river on a hot day especially on a day as hot as that!

After spending some time enjoying the cool waters, we got out and were about to start walking, when a villager approached us and asked us for the time. It was around 3:30 p.m.; I had picked up a bit of Tamil by then, so I had no problem in conveying the '3' part in Tamil but the '30' part proved to be a challenge. I tried to explain it to him through hand signals and a multitude of other ways, but he just looked at me with his eyebrows raised. Just when I was wondering if I should perhaps write it down for him, he burst out laughing. Now it was my turn to look at him with raised eyebrows. Still bubbling with mirth, he asked me in perfect English, "Is it 3:30?" I felt so embarrassed that I just nodded my head sheepishly and walked on.

"That was pretty bad. Thankfully, he didn't seem offended by what I did," I said.

"That was pretty stupid of you. You assumed that since he was a villager, he could only understand the regional language," Sri chided. "Classic case of Stereotyping."

Sam had a different point of view. "While it may be true in many cases, stereotyping in itself isn't bad. It is a natural practice of the mind to reduce complexity and to categorise things into easily identifiable groups. Like how we categorise tigers, lions etc. into big cats. Once you see a big cat, you pretty much know big cat, sharp teeth, run!

Whether we like it or not, the unconscious brain will continue creating them. What we can do is acknowledge that we carry them and ensure that they cause no harm."

It was easy, walking in the shade of the trees next to the river and I actually forgot all about my aching limbs. I hummed a few songs as we walked, and for once Sam and Sri didn't get into any arguments. They say that time flies when you do something that you enjoy. It was the same in our case and we *sailed* along the route and reached Erode in just a couple of hours.

As I sat in our hotel room that night, I started thinking about the experiences I had on this journey and how they had affected me. The most significant change was that I had started *praying* in the temples that we visited in the last few days. When I started this journey, I was doubtful, questioning the rationale. That however had changed along the way and I was now opening up my heart in temples and praying. Perhaps it was due to the experience I had in the temple, when I was reading the *Chalisa* or perhaps, it was because of the people we had encountered – good people who went out of their way to help a stranger, people who offered us food and shelter even when they had little for themselves. Whatever be the case, I still needed something more concrete to *believe*.

Day 24: The first sign you can't explain. The second sign you can't ignore. The third sign you....

Location: Erode, Tamil Nadu

Day 24 of our trip started auspiciously with us running into Lord Hanuman himself. Actually, it was a young boy dressed up as the Lord. He had the full outfit on – facemask, green paint, a *Gada*, a long tail, and leaves all over his body. We were talking to him when his army turned up – a gang of four boys. Once they noticed that I was carrying a camera, it became quite a rumpus. First, they made weird faces and we clicked some snaps after which they climbed some trees and swung around the branches for a few more snaps. Then they climbed back down and danced around us making ridiculously funny faces, until we could no longer control ourselves and burst out in laughter. After monkeying around for a good thirty minutes, the gang relieved us of almost all of our chocolate bars and left, still giggling quite gleefully.

After they left, I wondered if running into a kid dressed as Lord Hanuman was a sign or if I was looking too hard for one. I wasn't actually sure these days. That's the problem with events like these – to the believing eye they are signs, whereas to the sceptic they are just coincidences.

"Coincidence is God's way of remaining anonymous."- Albert Einstein

We planned to push hard to cover the forty kilometres from Erode to Kangayam by the end of the day. Thankfully, it was a pleasant day with plenty of clouds and the route passed through several plantations making the walk quite enjoyable. We walked quickly and by 12 noon, we had covered a distance of sixteen kilometres and decided to take a break at a coconut farm. I settled down under a tree and opened a book, while Sam and Sri decided to take a nap. While I was reading, a guy stopped his motorcycle and walked over. He spoke good Hindi, so we started talking about the weather and other general topics. He then pulled out a packet of biscuits and offered them to me. I was debating whether I should accept food from a complete stranger, when I felt something crawling up my foot. For a moment, I panicked, thinking that it was a snake only to find something worse; it was the stranger rubbing his foot against mine. That left no doubt as to whether I should accept the biscuits or not. I freaked out, jumped up, hurled the choicest of abuses that came to my mind, and chased him away. Unfortunately, it was too late. *Murphy's Law* was already in play.

"Please tell me that I wasn't imagining things," Sam said, with a huge grin.

"What did I miss?" Sri asked innocently.

"See that guy running away. That guy tried to seduce our dear friend."

"Seduce? Don't exaggerate. He offered me a packet of biscuits and tried to sit a little too close for comfort," I said.

"So you are worth a grand total of **one** packet of biscuits huh! Hahaha."

"I guess we don't need to worry about money for food anymore Sam. We can trade this one in whenever we feel hungry."

"Screw you guys," was all I could respond with.

"Naah, you're barking up the wrong tree. That guy left already. Do you want us to call him back?" Sam asked.

I just started walking again, instead of bothering to answer Sam. After walking for an hour, I started experiencing a dull pain in my foot. I thought about stopping for a while, but quickly realised it would be an exercise in futility. We still had a long way to go and if we stopped every time my feet became sore or ached, we would never get anywhere. Besides, there was no way we could go on a journey this long and not experience any pain. Pain would always be a part of the journey and I just had to get used to it. I plugged my headset into my phone and put on some music, hoping it would help deal with the pain. After trying out different songs, I realised that *slow music* seemed to be most effective so I walked on with *Oasis, Kishore Kumar, Switchfoot, Blink 182, The Who, The Doors, RHCP, Gorillaz, Beach Boys, and Rafi* keeping me company.

In addition to helping me deal with the pain, the music also helped drown out the *noise*. It was a relief to be walking without having to listen to the doubt in my head, as well as the incessant chatter between Sam and Sri. For nearly thirty kilometres, I walked – just my music and me. After that, I noticed that there was no pain anymore; my legs went numb. The pain had gone away and in its place, there was an overwhelming feeling of tiredness. All I could think of was resting, but I knew that if I sat down, there would be no getting up again. I just had to beat the pain and fatigue **once,** and that would give me the confidence needed to finish this journey else, I would end up quitting every time I felt tired. In the journey ahead, we had planned to cover over forty kilometres every day so I had to get used to walking that distance daily.

Noticing my discomfort Sam and Sri tried to help. They told stories and joked about the things we would do once we got back home. We counted road markers, trees, and even footsteps. Sam ranted at everyone and everything, while Sri delivered a sermon, and I hummed tunes to the point of annoying myself. It was all we could do to keep ourselves going, but it worked and we somehow managed to reach our destination. It had been a long day, in which we had covered around forty-two kilometres. We ended up at the Kangayam central bus stand at 9 p.m., dead tired and my body refusing to move another inch.

From Kangayam, we caught a bus to Tirupur to visit the Tirupur Tirupati temple (off route) and managed to drag ourselves to the nearest lodge and check in. The worst and the most tedious task for me always started after the walking ended – washing clothes. Since I was only carrying two shirts on this journey, I had to wash my clothes every day, especially if we planned to visit a temple the next day. On days like these, I actually looked forward to the walking rather than the washing.

Day 25: Man is least himself when he talks in his own person. Give him a mask, and he will tell you the truth

Location: Tirupur, Tamil Nadu

Tirupur is a business hub and is one of the largest textile markets in India. As expected, there were clothing stores as far as the eye could see in every direction. Considering that with only two shirts in my backpack, I felt like *Vikram* carrying *Betaal,* shopping was definitely out of the question.

After visiting the Tirupur Tirupati temple, we headed back to Kangayam and began the thirty-kilometre walk to Dharapuram. There were plenty of fenced off farms along the way and we kept jumping over the fences and walking until we were stopped by the farmers. Though they acted gruff initially, once they calmed down, they were kind enough to let us through, and some of them even invited us to lunch. Eventually, we walked into an area where the farms were small and were separated by huge barbed wire fences. All we could see was miles and miles of barbed wire.

The sight of barbed wires brought awake the master storyteller in Sri, "Do you guys know what happened when the Europeans sailed to America and met the Native Americans for the first time? They asked the natives if they could purchase some land and were met with derisive laughter. The natives didn't understand the concept of owning land; they held it immeasurable, *unownable,* and essentially as a gift for everybody to enjoy. The land was vast and free for all to use."

"Interesting, I'm sure our land mafia would have had a blast there!" Sam exclaimed.

"Well, I for one agree with the Native Americans. How can an individual 'own' land? It is a natural resource like water or air. I have always believed that a community based ownership of natural resources is better."

"You commie bastard! Every heard of USSR? Actually, take any communist country in the world. They all talk about 'sharing wealth and natural resources'. It's all very utopian when communists talk, but we all know where it actually ends," Sam responded.

"And democracy is doing so much good for you."

"Well, at least we have our basic rights and freedom," I said, butting into the conversation.

"Hah. That's just an illusion my friend; you only have them till they aren't trodden on. Think about it, just standing here in the middle of nowhere, we are probably breaking some law, made years ago. So if the government really wants to screw us over, they can invoke some archaic law, take us into custody and well, that's good-bye to your so called 'basic rights and freedom'. Democracy offers the illusion of control and that is why you embrace it. Anarchy is the one true solution," Sam said.

"Seriously? You can't be that stupid…"

I decided that I heard enough of the idiotic conversation. I had enough to deal with as it was. "Can the both of you just shut up and get back to the road. Considering the number of barbed wire fences we are jumping over or crawling under, it feels like we are escaping from a German POW camp."

We headed back to the road and started following it. Walking along a road certainly had its advantages – availability of food and water being one, and ease of walking being another. We stopped for lunch at a *dhaba* and had some delicious chicken, *palak paneer,* and *rotis.* We had been lucky in terms of food. We had eaten the most amazing food in shacks and *dhabas* and none of us had ended up sick. Considering the number of kilometres we were walking, I guess we could probably have eaten rocks and still not fallen sick.

It was yet another hot day and we had to take plenty of breaks to rest and rehydrate. I was getting used to the walking and was definitely much better off than the early days of the trip. After walking for a few hours, we took a break and munched on a couple of energy bars. After we were done, I got up too quickly and ended up pulling a muscle in my calf. I tried stretching it out and applied some balm but it didn't help. I tried walking it off, but there was a niggling pain whenever I took a step. This journey was definitely taking its toll on me. Sam and Sri were wondering if I would give up again but they needn't have worried. I knew what had to be done and there was no turning back anymore. I pushed on stubbornly, despite the pain and we made decent time. I had my mind made up that I would finish this journey, even on one leg if it was required. Eventually, we got into Dharapuram and checked into a hotel at 6 p.m., with my leg killing me. Being stubborn had its perks and downsides.

Day 26: All animals are equal, but some animals are more equal than others

Location: Dharapuram, Tamil Nadu

I woke up in the morning and spent a few minutes just lying on the bed and staring at the ceiling fan. The pain in my leg seemed to have disappeared, but as soon as I put some weight on it, the pain returned with a vengeance and I yelped out loud. I had pushed myself too hard, but that's just the way I was. I had only two modes of existence, 1) *Squirrel* mode – constantly on the move and doing something or, 2) *Sloth* mode - where I didn't do anything except sleep, browse the net, or read a book. I had tried several times, but I still hadn't quite managed to strike a balance in my life. I figured it was still better than being in only one of these modes throughout one's life.

Dharapuram was an important place in the journey as it had ten ancient statues of Hanuman in temples spread across the place. A quick shower later, we headed to the Kadu Hanumantharaya temple, which was the most famous of the Hanuman temples in Dharapuram. When we arrived at the temple, there was a VIP with a huge posse of security guards, so lesser mortals like us had to wait outside for him to be done. Such a pity, when a man fears for his life so much that he cannot live it freely. After the boss man left, we had a good darshan and talked to a priest regarding the locations of the other nine temples. He told us of one temple that he knew which had two statues of Hanuman – the Uttara Veera Raghava Perumal.

The Uttara Veera Raghava Perumal was a temple dedicated to Lord Murugan and had two Anjaneya statues guarding it. One of the statues was of *Veera Anjanair*, the other was of *Koottai Vaas Anjanair*, and both of them were around three thousand years old. The priest at the temple was extremely nice and helpful – he pointed out the various nuances of the idols, proceeded to recite the story of Lord Hanuman's journey to Lanka, and finally gave us directions to three other Hanuman temples in Dharapuram. Just as we were about thank him and leave, he mentioned something quite interesting. According to legend, the *Pandavas* had spent a year of their *Vanvas* in the Uttara Raghava temple itself. I didn't even know that the *Pandavas* had come so far down south during their exile!

We visited the three other statues that the priest told us about and then tried to find out the location of the remaining four statues, but nobody seemed to know anything about them. We spent half a day running around trying to find any information about these statues, but to no avail. We had a large map of the area on which we had marked the locations of the temples, but even when we showed this to people, no one was able to help us. Exhausted, we finally dragged ourselves back to the bus stand to catch a bus back to our hotel. An hour later, when we finally got a bus, the conductor refused to change a Rs. 100 note and asked us to get off. As my thoughts wavered between despair at the situation and anger at the conductor, a stranger came to my rescue. He chided the conductor for being so indifferent and paid our fare with a smile. That random act of kindness cleared my mind of all the negativity and brought a cheer to all of us. We had experienced a lot of such kindness on this trip and realized that the little things do make a big difference.

"I alone cannot change the world, but I can cast a stone across the waters to create many ripples." - Mother Teresa.

Back in Dharapuram, we settled down in our room, which for a change was comfortable. Since the journey was planned on a slim budget, most of the places we ended up staying in were borderline shady. This one however was well maintained despite being quite cheap. I settled down on the clean bed and started to relax, but with the guys around that was never really a possibility.

As usual, after he was comfortable, Sam started complaining, "Boy was it hot today! I thought this was the monsoon season. Where the hell are the rains?"

"It most definitely was. Look at that tan on our hero's face," Sri said. "Your parents are definitely not going to like this. I don't want to be around when they meet us."

"Eh?" I said, a little surprised.

"Well, they were getting ready to play matchmaker and find you a *nice homely* girl, but you ran away on this journey. Now you look like a burnt crow. No amount of fairness cream can save you now. Ayyo, who will marry such a boy," Sri said, tongue-in-cheek.

"Bad dog!" Sam exclaimed.

"Oh shut up. I don't need my parents to find me a match. I can manage to find one on my own," I said, a little defensively.

"Ha ha ha. Right, we know how well you have managed on your own."

"Maybe I should teach him some of my moves. Success guaranteed!" Sam boasted.

"For starters, I didn't run away on this journey and secondly, what moves? The one where you were on a date with a lizard up your pants or the one in which the girl ended up with a broken wrist?"

Sam knew when he was beaten and backed down, "Peace brother, even though in my defence it wasn't my fault in either of those cases."

"It never is and Sri, have you even been on a date?"

"*Gharbad* weak. Mercy please. Big reward," Sri pleaded, and that was the end of that.

After we started from Coimbatore, I wasn't too concerned about looking for signs. I figured that I would see one when I was supposed to see it, even if it took longer than usual. The last sign had given me some amount of confidence; it seemed to indicate that we were on the right path and that I hadn't fucked up completely. Although the question of what it meant was still unclear, the fact that it was there was more than enough for me to continue onwards.

Day 27: The dominant primordial beast was strong...

Location: Dharapuram, Tamil Nadu

The next morning, we were on the road to Palani to visit the Palani Hill temple. For a change, the weather was amazing and we had a strong wind at our backs, helping us along. We could see the cloud covered peaks of Kodaikanal in the distance – beautiful and enticing. We walked along, watching the wind blow through the fields – wave after wave and for a few minutes, the fields resembled the most beautiful of seas. It was a scene of indescribable beauty and was our moment of inspiration. Every trekker experiences these moments and this is what drives them forward; despite all the hardships, these singular moments of beauty and awe make it worth all the effort.

Walking was a cinch in these conditions and I didn't feel the weight of the pack, even after walking several kilometres. More than the good weather, it was probably the fact that we felt at one with our surroundings, which made it easier for us to walk. It was similar in the case of the section along the river. Either way, it just goes to show how much of a part our mind played in the pain and suffering we underwent.

We continued our walk and made good time thanks to the good weather and our newfound cheer. We were around five kilometres from Palani, when a man on a *Chetak* scooter (the quintessential Indian family steed upon which entire families would perform acts of daredevilry to get around!) stopped next to us. He introduced himself as Mahesh, a cook who made *Halwa* for the Palani temple. Apparently, he had seen us in the morning, walking from Dharapuram, and was shocked to know that we had walked the entire way. "Why not take a bus?" he asked and we were forced to explain our journey to him. He was very happy to hear about it as he was a devotee of Lord Hanuman. He insisted on taking us to Palani and as an incentive promised to tell us the story of Palani.

"A long long time ago, Lord Shiva and Parvati Devi were presented with the Pazham (fruit of wisdom) by Sage Narada. He wanted to split the fruit between his sons Ganesha and Murugan, but was advised against cutting the fruit. Faced with this dilemma, he decided that he would gift the fruit of wisdom to the son, who circled the world thrice and returned first. Murugan, immediately hopped on his peacock, circled the world thrice and came back. Upon his return, he found Ganesha happily eating the fruit of wisdom! While Murugan was away, Ganesha had simply circled Lord Shiva and Parvati Devi thrice, claiming that his parents (Shiva and Shakti) were the world. Impressed by Ganesha's wisdom, Lord Shiva had gifted him the fruit. Overcome with anger, Murugan left his heavenly abode and came down to earth. Later, Lord Shiva pacified Murugan by explaining that one need not seek the fruit of wisdom, as all wisdom was within oneself. From then on, the place came to be known as 'Pazham-nee' or 'Palani', meaning, "You are (nee) the fruit of wisdom (Pazham)". Murugan settled on the hill and continues to reside here and hence Palani is considered to be a very auspicious place."

That simple story gave me quite a lot to think about regarding my own journey. Here I was, walking thousands of kilometres, searching for *'answers or wisdom'* about my faith and I hear a story about the futility of searching for wisdom. Maybe whatever 'answers or wisdom' I was searching for were within me; I just had to recognize them. I realized that I carried the belief that my faith would sort of just appear, but maybe I had to actually think about it to make any progress. That would be troublesome to say the least.

Once in Palani, we got into a lodge, showered and headed towards the temple. The Palani temple is the most famous of Murugan temples in India and is considered as one of the six earthly abodes of Lord Murugan. There was a series of stairs to walk up to the temple and along the way, we encountered every possible travel scam that could be imagined. A brief sample:

1) I apply sacred ash to your forehead. Pay me.
2) I get you special *Darshan*. Pay me.

3) I blessed you and gave you *Aarti.* Pay me.
4) I see you looking at my beads. Pay me.
5) We keep your bags and footwear safe…safe from you!

Like shy brides, we kept our heads down and ignored their calls. We reached the temple just in time for the Golden chariot darshan and managed to get a couple of good photographs of the procession. The statue of *Cinnakumarar* (Murugan) was placed on a golden peacock and then loaded on to a beautiful golden chariot. The chariot was taken around the temple by the priests, while the rest of us followed, chanting the Lord's name. As the crowd chanted, we could feel a certain connection, a shared energy, and euphoria. At the end of the puja, the priest distributed *Prasad* to all the devotees.

It reminded me of my younger experiences with prayer and faith. Days with long daily pujas, where I would sit in my father's lap and daydream, as he chanted various *mantras*. There was certainly something soothing about the whole experience of sitting there and listening to him, but that wasn't what drew me to prayer; it was all about the sweets. All I could think of was when he would finish and I could eat the sweet offerings prepared for the Gods. I was too young to appreciate the feeling then, but now I did, and it brought a smile to my face.

Day 28: Wugga, wugga, gaijin – it's go time!

Location: Palani, Tamil Nadu

The next morning, we returned to the temple and spent time looking at the idols and the temple architecture. The temple offered panoramic views of the Palani hills and we could see the thick cloud cover and green forests, enticing us. The view got us all fired up and we headed to the Forest office for trekking permits from Palani to Kodaikanal. We had plotted the route out by looking at various satellite maps and it ran along a rivulet from the Palar dam, almost all the way to Kodai.

Once we got to the forest office, nobody had a clue about the permits. It appeared as if no one had asked for permits in many years, so no one even knew the correct process to issue us permits. In true bureaucratic style, instead of trying to find a solution, they took the easy way out and flatly denied us the permits. Since we were desperate and had all the time in the world, we persisted with our demands, *"Hamari maange puri karo, jangal mein mangal karne do. Trekker union zindabad, sloth bears zindabad, animal rights zindabad, forest office down down..."* They eventually got sick of our badgering and came up with another classic bureaucratic solution – dump the problem on someone else. They asked us to go to the forest office in Dindigul and get the permits there. This wasn't the first time that we had faced this problem. In fact, this was actually the norm rather than the exception. There was a thin line between regulation and oppression. They weren't supposed to lock up all the forests all the time. We decided to ignore the rules and worry about it, if we were caught. Seriously, what could go wrong?

It was a twelve-kilometre walk to the Palar dam, which was the starting point of the trek. The road we were on, had trees on both sides and ran close to several farms and plantations. We planned to walk along the road until we were close to Palar dam and then cut across to our planned route. However, once we were near the dam, we ran into a problem we hadn't quite anticipated – a forest check post with a lone guard.

As soon as he spotted us, he beckoned us over. He must have suspected that we were poachers or Naxalites, because he asked us to put our hands up, as we approached him. He then made us take off our backpacks and went through the contents carefully. Only after a thorough search was he convinced that we weren't Naxalites, and started asking questions:

"What are you doing here?" he asked.

"I am a research associate working on a project…" I lied, hoping to convince him to let us through.

"Liar liar. Pants on fire!" Sam whispered.

"Shut up and let the man lie in peace," Sri whispered.

The forest guard continued his questioning, "Do you have permission?"

I decided to tell a half-truth hoping that it would get us through, "I talked to the officer in Palani."

The guard was a no nonsense guy, "Show me the permit slip," he said.

"The Forest officer asked me to inform you at the check post as we passed."

"No slip. No entry."

"Ok. I am just going to follow the road."

"Not allowed," was his response.

"According to the Forest Act of 1942…"

"Not allowed."

"You have no right to stop me."

"Not allowed."

"It's my choice and I am going on ahead. The Act is pretty clear that I can go through."

"I will arrest you and detain you. Explain the Act to my superior."

"@#$@$$."

Although he didn't help in the least, Sam had to be a smart-ass, "That went well. Do you want to explain any other Act to him as well? He seems to be quite receptive."

We realised that it was pointless to argue, especially with an unreasonable man and his gun, so we decided to just sneak past him. We acted disappointed and told the guard that we would catch the bus to Kodaikanal. We then walked back three hundred metres, out of sight of the forest guard and got off the road. We cut through the thick bushes and managed to sneak past the forest check post. Soon, we were able to find the trail and on our way to Kodaikanal. Half a kilometre ahead, we ran straight into another Forest guard.

"What are you doing here?

Do you have permission?"

Long story short, our sneaky ninja skills weren't up to the mark and we soon found ourselves escorted out of the forest range and sitting in a bus bound for Kodaikanal. The forest guard even asked some of our fellow travellers to keep an eye on us and make sure that we got down only at Kodaikanal and not before it. The bus slowly made its way along the winding road amidst the thick green forests, while I stared outside the window morosely. A kind soul noticed this and offered me his seat next to the window. I started clicking photos, all the while imagining walking through the forests.

We reached Kodaikanal by 5 p.m., and were immediately surrounded by several *coyotes,* who offered to get us everything from a toothbrush to the Taj Mahal. We ignored their polite and not so polite offers and headed to the forest department and the tourism office for information on the treks around Kodaikanal. It was quite late and both the offices were closed, so we headed towards Coaker's walk and checked into the Greenlands Hostel. Since it was off-season, we managed to get a room with an unobstructed view of Palani and its surrounding plains.

Day 29: When life gives you lemons, squirt it in somebody's eye and run like hell

Location: Kodaikanal, Tamil Nadu

Kodai – the princess of hill stations looked every bit like one at dawn. A thin mist hung in the air, which enveloped everything and danced through the trees whenever there was a breeze. The entire town was full of greenery; trees, ferns, and shrubs grew out of every imaginable place and sometimes even the unimaginable ones. Add to this a thick cloud cover that blocked out the sun and the weather was perfect to settle down with a hot drink and a good book.

We sat in the patio relaxing until Sam got restless and started hounding us to head out. Eventually, we gave in and went to Coaker's walk, to catch the views. Coaker's walk is a one kilometre paved pathway, which is supposed to offer a panoramic view of the plains. We however, didn't see jackshit; the mist completely blocked out the view and all we could see was the disappointed faces of other tourists.

Disappointed, we headed towards the forest office hoping for better luck there. Fortunately, the folks at this forest office knew how to issue permits for trekking and we were done with the process within thirty minutes. Once we were done with the permits, we had nothing to do so we headed to a café. As I had my hot chocolate, a wave of melancholy spread over me. It seemed like one of those days in which life just goes nowhere. You don't feel like doing anything and just sit and wait for the day to end. As I ordered more hot chocolate to kill time, Sri came up with an idea.

"You know what. Let's do what the '*tourists*' do. Let's catch a cab and visit the '*touristy*' spots in town."

"You have got to be kidding me. You seriously want to go on a tourist run?" Sam asked incredulously.

"I know you hate them, but it's not like they are always bad."

"Let me remind you why we avoid tourist runs. Because **every** time we try one, the guides take it upon themselves to eat all the crap they can find in the area, vomit it out, eat it again and crap the living shit out on our faces. And you ask me why."

Sam was on a roll, "Do you remember Andaman? The guides recommended doing the Ross Island trip and the Jarwa trip. The Jarwa trip started at 5 a.m., with a bus full of families eating chips and farting at every bump on the road. That continued for 3 hours until we stopped for breakfast, after which all I could smell was frikkin omelette farts the rest of the damn way. We then passed through the jungle, where we saw a *native* in his *nothing-special-don't-look-at-me-yellow-shorts* and the entire bus rushed to look at the savage. It was disgusting how people reacted and the names they called him. To top it all off, we didn't even get to see Parrot island. Ideally, we should have just stayed overnight at Parrot island to see the parrots and then taken a boat to Port Blair, the next day. Yeah, that's what I call a perfectly planned tour."

I agreed with what Sam was saying, "Yeah, even Ross Island was a waste of time. It's good that we ditched the guide and headed to Neil and Havelock. Andaman was all about the snorkelling, scuba, and swimming with elephants and crocodiles!"

"Andaman, Sikkim, Kerala, MP, every time we tried an organized tour, we regretted it. It wasn't just one problem, it was everything – timings, money, places etc. You name it and they screw it up!"

Sri had heard enough, "Well, here is a better idea for the both of you. Shut up and stay in the room. You guys never do what I want to do. Maybe I should just leave."

With the threat of a boycott and with no counter proposal, we were left with no choice but to go with him, so off we went looking for a taxi. We found one who was willing to take us to twelve places around Kodai including Pillar rocks, the Devil's kitchen, Green

Valley View, and the Kurinjiandavar temple for eight hundred bucks. The guy must have watched *The Transporter* one too many times because as soon as we got into the van, he zoomed off tearing through corners like there was no tomorrow. We clung onto whatever we could grab and held on for dear life. Several harrowing minutes later, we arrived at our first stop, the Kurinjiandavar temple.

The temple is dedicated to Sri Kurinji Easwaran (Lord Murugan) and is located at the edge of a cliff. It is named after the *Kurinji* flowers that bloom here once every 12 years. The temple offered amazing views of both Palani and Kodai and was the only place where we managed to see anything before the mist stepped in and sent us on our way.

From there on, the tour turned out to be an unmitigated disaster. We couldn't enjoy a single view of the surrounding valleys and forests as all the touristy view-points were fenced off; everything even remotely near a cliff had been fenced to prevent people from committing suicide. It didn't matter that there were a thousand other places to jump off from. Whatever wasn't fenced off was impossible to see thanks to the thick mist. We couldn't see Pillar rocks at all or Devil's kitchen and we just about managed to catch the Green Valley view. The only upside (again) were the monkeys at Green Valley, which were a real playful lot and had one hell of a party – stealing people's caps, drinks, snacks and bags and taunting them.

Sam ribbed Sri all through the tour, while Sri tried to keep himself calm with his kitten chants. After a few hours of Sam's merciless taunting, Sri just fell silent and stopped talking to us. We finished the rest of the organized tour in silence and headed back to the forest office to inform them of our decision to get out of Kodai first thing in the morning. Just one guided tour and we were ready to skip town.

Day 30: Madness? This is Sparta!

Location: Kodaikanal, Tamil Nadu

The day started painfully for me yet again. I was attempting to further decrease the weight of my backpack by cutting off the handle of my toothbrush. *(Why do toothbrushes have such long handles anyway?)* As the knife cut through the toothbrush's handle, I was too slow in moving my hand away and ended up splitting the webbing between my fingers. It wasn't a very deep cut, but it was painful and I felt stupid in hindsight. Hindsight was such a bitch, especially since she kept rubbing it in.

By the time I had patched up my hand, the guide from the forest department arrived at the hotel. His name was Nathan and he explained the trek guidelines as any good guide should. Since we were anxious to get out of Kodai, we skipped breakfast and headed to the starting point of the trek. The trek was supposed to be sixteen kilometres long and would take us through Vellagavi village and end at Periyakulam.

The trail passed through deep valleys and circled around several mountains covered with lush Shola forests ensuring that there was always an amazing view or sight to see. Thanks to the thick forest cover, it was cool and all of us trekked along happily. For a 52-year-old chain smoker, Nathan was insanely fit and had inhuman levels of stamina. We continued down the valley without taking many breaks, only stopping a couple of times to take in the spectacular views of the plains and the surrounding areas below us.

By 10 a.m., we were at Vellagavi village at which point God decided we were having way too much fun and turned the heat up. We had been walking for around three and a half hours by then and the effects of our skipping breakfast started to show. Luckily, a kind soul invited us to his house and offered us tea and biscuits. We offered to pay, but he politely waved us off, leaving us feeling guilty for offering it in the first place. Travellers encounter this behaviour a lot and it takes a while to get used to the idea that the world doesn't always revolve around money.

The next part of the trek was almost entirely downhill and it slowly but surely took its toll on our knees. When trekking uphill we could at least lean forward, but try doing this downhill and we were sure of a tumble. We had to lean back to arrest any momentum, which created a lot of pressure on my knees and my feet. I still soldiered on, despite the hot sun blazing down on our backs. To make matters worse, the vegetation changed, from thick forests that shielded us from the sun to a scrub forest of sorts. We sweated bullets, thanks to the hard work and heat, and no amount of water seemed to sate our thirst.

After a couple of hours of trekking without any breaks, my legs felt like jelly. They wobbled with every step and I had to spend increasing amounts of energy to keep myself stable. Nathan led the way and expected us to tell him when we needed a break. However, there was a problem with that idea – I viewed every trek as a battle, hence asking for a break was a sign of cowardice and weakness. I just couldn't bring myself to ask for a break no matter how shitty I felt, so onward we went at break neck speed.

We eventually completed our trek by 12 noon, had lunch, and bid farewell to Nathan. After our detour at Dharapuram to visit Palani and Kodai, we now headed back onto the original route to Dindigul. A quick bus ride later, we arrived at Dindigul, and checked into a hotel. We decided to relax for the rest of the day, as we were completely exhausted. It was then that I realized that I had run out of things to read. Since I had a reason and since Sam was still restless, we forced the *tyranny of majority* on Sri and headed out to buy a few books and visit the Dindigul fort. The whole idea reeked of stupidity, since we were already dog-tired after the trek. However, Masochism 101 seemed to be the theme of the day, so off we went.

After a visit to the fort, we went looking for a bookshop. We managed to find one after thirty minutes of walking. Ask anyone for directions and it was always *seedha* and *thoda door*. Once there, we realised that we had no money on us and had to find an ATM. The nearest ATM was another two kilometres away and was also *seedha* and *thoda door*. Since we couldn't get an auto-rickshaw, we had to walk there and then all the way back. I could swear that the *squirrels* wanted me dead.

After walking for what felt like ten thousand kilometres, I picked up *Blink* and *Heart of Darkness*. An hour later, we were back at the hotel and sure as you know it, I ended up sick. I started puking and felt feeble. Was it just the exhaustion or something I ate? I wasn't sure, but I was too tired to get up and go to a hospital. I hadn't felt so tired since... oh yeah, the day before. I would wrap up...zzzzzzz.

Day 31: Carnivores have all the fun!

Location: Dindigul, Tamil Nadu

I woke up feeling weak, nauseous, and with one hell of a cramp. That's when I realised that I was suffering from heat exhaustion. I had pushed too hard the previous day and had lost an unhealthy amount of body salts, thus causing the heat cramp. I took some ORS and multivitamins, ate a couple of bananas and went back to bed. I woke up after a few hours feeling much better. Being great friends, Sam and Sri cracked all sorts of jokes about my condition. After a couple of hours of incessant ragging, I figured that it would be better to get out of bed and visit the Nadupatti Anjaneyar temple, as opposed to listening to them for the rest of the day.

As with all temples we had visited so far, there was an interesting legend behind the origins of this temple as well. During the Ramayana war, Indrajit, the most valiant of Ravana's sons, wounded Lord Lakshman. Noticing how critical the wounds were, Jambavanta, the king of bears asked Lord Hanuman to fetch four medicinal herbs (*Mrita Sanjeevani, Vishalyakarani, Suvarnakarani,* and *Sandhani*) from the *Rishabha* Mountain in the Himalayas. Hanuman flew all the way to the Himalayas, but could not identify the herbs, so he decided to pick up the entire mountain and fly back with it to Lanka. On the way back, he decided to take a break since carrying a mountain is no easy work even for a god. Legend says that this was the place where he rested for a while before resuming his journey back to Lanka. Hence, the idol in the temple depicts him carrying a mountain.

This was interesting because there was another Ramayana legend associated with this area – that the Sirumalai peaks are a part of the *Rishabha* Mountain that Lord Hanuman was carrying. In fact, medicinal herbs are extracted from those peaks even to this day. The priest in the temple mentioned that the river rises up and overflows almost every year during the monsoons. When that happens, the temple is partially submerged and hence the idol in the temple was known as *Jalakanta Anjaneyar, Jala* meaning water in a bunch of languages.

Later that evening, back in Dindigul, we went to eat the famous Dindigul Biryani at 'Venu Biryani'. A polite waiter ushered us in quickly and seated us at a table.

"Could you get us some Dindigul Biryani please?" I asked.

"Sure Sir. You don't look like you are from around here. I'm sure you will enjoy our amazing Biryani," the waiter replied.

Sam couldn't keep his big mouth shut, "Well, we have eaten the legendary Hyderabad Biryani several times. Can your Biryani be better than that?"

"Really? Did you have to challenge him?" Sri whispered.

"Yes. Now he is going to take it personally and make sure the Biryani tastes better. I just made it an ego trip."

"As long as he doesn't spit in it!" I said.

"Trust more. Talk less," was Sri's reply.

The waiter rushed to the kitchen and said, "Get one *special* Biryani in quick time. It's Hyderabad vs. Dindigul!"

We were served the Biryani within ten minutes and the waiter watched as we dug into it; soon a couple of his fellow workers joined him. At this point, we were relishing the Biryani; the mutton was cooked perfectly (not too chewy and not too soft) and the rice was also well done. The major difference was in the variety of rice used and the fact that they used plenty of spices. I personally liked the Hyderabadi version better. Comparisons weren't probably apt here though, as this was supposed to be a different variation of the dish but try telling that to the mob that had built up behind us!

We were in a soup now and we did not want to hurt anybody's feelings through an unfair comparison. Tell the truth and hurt people and our poor bones or lie and be nice. We all face this situation sometimes and we generally choose to tell the white lie. I always believed this was wrong and truth was the ultimate good, until someone stuck me with this poser from *Kantian ethics* – Let's say there was a murderer looking for his next victim. You knew where the target was and as luck would have it, the murderer asks you. How do you answer? Remember that staying silent is the same as lying. What was right and what was wrong?

While we were debating that conundrum, we finished eating and the mob came up and asked us how it was. I exclaimed, "Sooper" and everybody was happy and we all went our merry ways. Thankfully, nobody brought up a comparison. Phew! That was a close shave, no thanks to Sam and his big mouth.

We headed back and crashed after a long day for some much needed rest. It wasn't meant to be – there was a police raid at 1 a.m.

"What are you doing?" the policeman asked rudely.

"I'm having an orgy with these two. What do you think I am doing at 1 a.m.?" was what came to mind. "Sleeping," was what I actually said.

"Go back to sleep," came the policeman's curt response.

"Could you ask him to get me a chocolate bar? I have the munchies," Sri mumbled.

Day 32: You talk to God, you're religious. God talks to you, you're psychotic.

Location: Dindigul, Tamil Nadu

"So, how is your madness today?" Sam asked. He seemed to be in a belligerent mood.

"What's wrong with you now?" I asked, taking the bait. After being with him for so long, I should have known better.

"I'm just curious as to the progress of your *faith hunt.* The squirrels in the attic settle down yet?"

"You make it sound as if I'm stark raving mad."

"Well, if you think about it, you have already made us walk nearly five hundred kilometres based on your dream."

"If that's what you think, then how would you explain the dream and the series of incidents that we had on this trip?"

"The dream was just a dream, nothing more nothing less and the incidents were just a bunch of coincidences, the only exception being the meditation one.

The mind is amazingly complex and has plenty of quirks, especially a believing mind. Plenty of people have willed them into madness. Saints, sadhus, and holy men have convinced themselves that the attainment of nirvana is through renunciation. Some psychopaths have actually seen their victims as demons and believed they were performing acts of good by murdering them.

In your case, you have willed yourself through your belief into unlocking something in your head, possibly a *chakra* gate."

"Whoa. Back up a little there. Did you just say that all the wise men in the world are insane?" Sri asked incredulously.

"Nope. I'm saying that they pretty much brainwashed themselves into thinking this is the truth and thus they are happy. It is possible to achieve nirvana through any activity, as long as you are thoroughly convinced about it yourself."

"Any activity?"

"Think about it. There are certain everyday activities that you enjoy so much that time just passes by without you noticing, like that cup of coffee with a newspaper or the walk in the park. Theoretically, it is possible to extend these activities for longer periods and thus achieve nirvana. Yup, even choking kittens would work," Sam said, with a wicked smile.

"That theory is really pushing it. In fact, it is pushing it so far that you don't even realize that the sign reads, 'Pull'. In all seriousness though, don't you think the dream was providing him with direction; direction on what he was supposed to do in life. His purpose?"

"I think that's poppycock. There is no such thing as purpose. It's just made up bullshit to keep people from realising the truth."

"Which is?"

"We've been through this before. The fact that we are responsible for our actions. Destiny is for cowards, who cannot accept it and blame others for their problems. People use destiny as an excuse to deny responsibility for their mistakes and lack of capability."

"Why are you here then?"

"I'm here on my own choosing – to have fun and to fulfil my duty as a friend. And trust me, I am having a lot of fun listening to your idiotic theories about purpose and destiny."

"You know what – there are some things that you just can't explain. You have to experience them and I hope that one day you will. We will continue this discussion then."

What an awesome way to start the day! With that pep talk from Sam, we headed off towards the Sirumalai hills. Since it was located in a reserve forest, this time we decided to take a bus instead of trying to ninja our way in. We were glad with our decision though, because it started raining heavily as soon as the bus started. It was still pouring when the bus reached the temple in Sirumalai. We jumped out and ran to the temple, but got drenched while taking our shoes off. You just can't win sometimes!

We entered the temple leaving puddles of water behind, but the kind priest didn't seem to mind it at all. He smiled at us and said that if we had any wishes, now was the time to ask. I wondered what I should wish for, maybe what everybody wished for – World *piece*! After we were done with our prayers, the priest locked up and left, leaving us to wait out the rain.

Suddenly, an old man walked in, offered his prayers, and started talking to us. He asked me what I was doing there and once I told him that I was walking along Lord Hanuman's route, from Hampi to Mahendragiri, we had the following conversation:

"Why are you doing this?" the old man asked.

"I had a dream that I was walking along Lord Hanuman's route and that's why I am doing this," I replied.

"Do you have a lot of these dreams?"

"A few, but not like this."

"What do you make of them?"

I hesitated for a few seconds, wondering if I should tell him what I really thought. There was something about the old man though, which made me open up and say what was on my mind since the morning. "I think they are signs of sorts," I said.

"Signs?" the old man asked, with an amused look on his face.

"I believe that life gives us signs on what we are supposed to be doing," Sri said, butting into the conversation.

"What happens if you don't follow them?"

"The signs are initially subtle, but keep getting stronger until you pick up on them. If you continue to ignore them, the signs stop and you get a harsh lesson from life. The trick therefore is to recognise the signs and change before they become lessons. Smart people pick them up earlier, while the obstinate or stupid ones learn in hindsight. That's what I have figured out so far," Sri said.

"Looks as if life figured you were too dumb to see signs, so it had to send you a dream," Sam whispered to me.

"What are the signs telling you now?" the old man asked me.

"Actually, not much in the last few days. I have so many doubts, doubts about the reason for the journey, whether I am doing it right, and if I can actually finish what I started," I replied.

"To achieve one's dreams, one must have great strength. Some of us are driven by the strength that we draw from our skill or wisdom, while others from their faith. Whichever it is, what matters is that we use this strength to overcome doubt and move forward towards our dreams."

"Are you saying that my journey makes sense?"

"All I am saying is that you follow your dreams. Purpose and achievement comes through that."

With that, the old man left as quickly as he had arrived, leaving us a little dumbfounded. I had an overwhelming feeling of déjà vu all through the conversation. Then it struck me - the reason I had the feeling was that the conversation was very similar to the thoughts from my dream; in fact, some of the thoughts and the words used to convey them were identical. It was then that I realised that I had incorrectly assumed that the voice I heard in the dream were my thoughts. Now that I had heard the old man's voice, there was no doubt that it was the same voice from my dream.

When the revelation hit me, I was stunned. A million thoughts rushed through my head. What was going on? How was this even possible? Was I hallucinating? I pinched myself to check and realised that I was most certainly awake. It wasn't possible and yet it had happened. I had been looking for signs all through the journey and had construed many incidents as signs, but when something like this hit me in square in the jaw, I found it impossible to believe, which was quite odd.

I told Sam and Sri about it and it gave us a lot to think about. Random old man walks into a temple in the middle of heavy rain, speaks perfect English, and imparts sage advice. Advice from a dream that I had months ago, which nobody knew of. There was no way we could write this off as coincidence. As usual, Sam attempted to come up with a logical explanation. He thought that since I was looking desperately for a sign, my mind played tricks on me and convinced me that the old man's words were the same as the ones from my dream. Even though he tried to be all rational and logical about it, I could see that he didn't seem too convinced either, especially since he knew the details of my dream as well. There was just too much in common to write it off as a quirk of my mind.

We sat in the temple and waited for the bus to return. Nobody said a word, but I could tell that we were all thinking of the same thing – how were the words from the old man and my dream the same? Was it just a ridiculously improbable coincidence or was it actually a sign? If it was a sign, where did it come from? Was Lord Hanuman actually giving us signs? Was that even possible?

Every person has a *tipping point,* after which he realises that the coincidences are actually signs. This was my tipping point, the point where I truly started to believe in impossible things.

With these thoughts for company, we caught a bus to the NH7 and started walking along it towards Madurai. After we had walked a few kilometres, it started to get dark. We wanted to setup camp before we ran out of light, so we entered a plantation off the highway, quickly cleared out an area, and unpacked the bivy.

Sam was generally distrustful of people, but in this trip, his misanthropy had reached new heights. He thought it was unsafe to let someone sneak up on us while we were asleep and decided to set up an early warning system. He stuck some sticks in the ground about half a foot off the ground and secured a rope around them. He then tied some bells to the rope. He figured that this would alert us as soon as someone walked into the rope. Sri hoped that the early warning system would work with animals as well, but knowing how smart they were, that was unlikely.

Day 33: I am the thing that goes bump in the night! I am the neurosis that requires a five-hundred-dollar-an-hour shrink!

Location: Random plantation off the National Highway

One thing that every person should do at least once in his or her life is spend a few days in the wilderness. Not a luxury camping trip, but a trip in which they cook, trek, navigate, and survive all by themselves. This causes a few major changes in perspective. Firstly, it ensures a better appreciation of nature and its beauty – the cool breeze blowing through the trees, birds chirping, animals going about their business, all of which you can never hope to experience in the city. Secondly, it helps us appreciate the luxuries in life, which we take for granted; every day convenience like readily available food, water, shelter, transport and even our own health. Most importantly, it helps in slowing down and understanding how to pace your life; rushing in a long trek (as I did) is going to get you nothing but weariness, same as in life. All of these help in leading happier and more satisfying lives.

"After that quick commercial break in which we disbursed unsolicited gyan, we now return to our regular broadcasting," Sam intoned.

Despite being dog tired, I didn't get much sleep and only managed to get some shut eye at around 4 a.m. We eventually 'woke up', had breakfast, and started on the long walk ahead of us. Since we were walking along the highway, we managed to walk around twenty-five kilometres before stopping for lunch.

One thing that a long walk always does is clear your head. That bill to be paid, the work that needs to be finished, the mail to be sent, that douche to talk to…everything goes out of your head. All you care about is the next step. It's like meditation, you start with a clean slate. It is a chance to think of new ideas, new philosophies, and of course new methods of idiocy. Out with the old and in with the new.

A long walk was exactly what I needed, especially after the previous day's incident. As we walked, my thoughts drifted towards the incident and how it affected everything. It was clear that someone up there was handing out signs, but to what end? Unless he had a plan, there wouldn't be a point in doling out signs. Was the plan pre-determined (aka destiny) or was it one made up on the fly? What were the benefits of both and what was the purpose? Was it nirvana? Was it like Sri said? Earlier, I was worrying about the existence of signs. Now that I had experienced one such sign, it only seemed to throw up more questions. Some people just can't be helped.

Meanwhile, the Sun decided to turn it up a few notches and it felt as if we were walking in an oven. After ten kilometres of walking in the blistering sun, we reached Samayanallur. There was no relief in sight; no shady groves or plantations, not even solitary trees; only a vast expanse of dusty land, where the sun bore down with its full wrath. We realised that we would burn ourselves out, if we continued walking in the heat, so we caught a bus and reached Mattutavani – Madurai Central Bus stand.

We checked into a hotel and a little later, headed out to find a barber. I needed a haircut and a shave; the way I looked right then, I could have been mistaken for a bear and shot! We looked around and found a barbershop at the bus stand itself. I was so tired that I fell asleep halfway through the haircut. I figured it wasn't an issue since I had already given the barber instructions. By the time I woke up, I went from looking like a furry bear to a plucked chicken.

"Do you like it?" the barber asked, quite pleased with his effort.

"Do you?" I asked.

"Uhh…" the barber said clearly puzzled.

"Since you cut it the way you liked, why bother asking me if I like it? You should be the one who likes it," I said.

"Your parents are going to be here in a couple of days and they are going to freak out!" Sri said.

"Thank you very much for the encouraging words, but why the hell didn't you guys wake me up when he was going *John Rambo* on my hair?"

"Well, we thought about it, but figured this outcome would be way more entertaining," Sam replied.

With friends like these who needed enemies.

Day 34 to 36: Who the hell do you think I am?!

Location: Madurai, Tamil Nadu

Since my family wasn't due in Madurai for another couple of days, we decided to continue walking and backtrack once they arrived. Over the next couple of days, we walked to Virudunagar and Sattur.

The days were hotter than ever, and we had to take longer and more frequent breaks. All the while, we kept drinking water and ORS to ensure none of us would get a heat stroke. I felt that a desert would have got an inferiority complex when compared to that place, and we actually considered the possibility of walking at dusk and dawn or at night as people do in deserts.

Just when we reached Sattur and decided to head back to Madurai, it started raining. Actually, it didn't just rain, it poured. It poured so hard that by the time we arrived in Madurai, it was completely flooded. We walked around the water-clogged streets trying to find a lodge and some food, but everything was closed. Tired, cold, and hungry. That was the last straw for Sri.

"You have got to be kidding me. We walk all this distance in the hot sun and now when we are done with the walking for a few days, it rains so hard that we can't even find food."

"Well, apparently the lord has an ironical sense of humour. Just enjoy it boys!" I exclaimed, weirdly elated.

"What's going on up there, dear God?" Sri asked, looking to the skies.

Sam loved the chaos though, "Now this is more like it. I was thinking this trip was getting a little stale and what do you know; it suddenly gets exciting. We are in a city that's flooding, with no food and no shelter. This is the beginning of the end."

"Now I'm definitely sure that you need professional help," Sri replied.

"Why? Just because I'm strong enough to survive any chaotic or disastrous situation?"

"No. It's because you look forward to it."

"Come on. You guys know the end of the world is coming. No matter how much we try, we cannot stop it. We tried to stop global warming; half the world doesn't even believe in it or doesn't care. We have killed off so many species that we have lost count. We are cruel to animals beyond imagination. Forget animals, we kill human beings with the same callousness. The end is nigh and you cannot stop it. We might as well accelerate it and enjoy the last few years."

"Aren't you due for your annual head check at Arkham?" I asked.

Day 37: Skadoosh

Location: Madurai, Tamil Nadu

We were awakened at 5 a.m., by the arrival of my parents and to my surprise my brother. My dad and brother could never stand the sight of anyone sleeping peacefully. They wouldn't ever directly wake you up though. Instead, they would just run around the room like foxes with their tails on fire, ensuring that you eventually get frustrated enough to get out of bed yourself. To cut a long story short, they ensured that we were all up and ready by 7 a.m. We caught a bus to Rameshwaram and arrived there at 1 p.m.

Along the way, we managed to get a decent view of the Pamban Bridge as the bus passed over it. The Pamban Bridge, at 2.3 kilometres is the second longest sea bridge in India and connects the mainland to Pamban Island, where the Sri Ramanathaswamy temple is located.

We started towards Dhanushkodi to see the *Sangam*, the confluence of the Indian Ocean and the Bay of Bengal. At Dhanushkodi, the sea on the east i.e. the Bay of Bengal side was calm, with almost no wave action (hence called *Pen Kadal* or Lady Sea), while the Indian Ocean towards the west was choppy and had rift currents running (hence called *Aan Kadal* or Male Sea). This was it; we were standing on Rama Setu, the bridge that Lord Rama had built to get to Sri Lanka. We looked at the horizon for Sri Lanka but that was wishful thinking.

On our way back, we visited the old town of Dhanushkodi, which still had remnants of a church and a railway station, which were destroyed in the 1964 cyclone. We also visited the Kothanda Ramasamy Temple (Vibheeshana Temple), where Lord Rama met Vibheeshana and coronated him as the ruler of Lanka. The story of the Ramayana and Vibheeshana is painted on the walls of this temple.

Our next stop was the *Jada Teertha,* the place where Lord Rama washed his *jada* (hair) to cleanse himself of his sins before returning to Ayodhya. The *Jada Teertham* is one of the prominent *Teerthas* in Rameshwaram. Legend has it that people who have a bath in these *Teerthas* are absolved of all their sins.

Since the fire-tailed foxes were up and about, as soon as we returned to town, we were coerced into visiting the temple for *Aarti* at 8 p.m. I was dead tired by the time we headed back and all I wanted to do was sleep. Sadly, that wasn't meant to be. The mosquitoes in Rameshwaram seemed to have taken it upon themselves to cleanse out my sins one drop at a time and kept me awake until 4 a.m.

Day 38: Carpe diem, seize the day boys, make your lives extraordinary.

Location: Rameshwaram, Tamil Nadu

The Ramanathaswamy temple is one of the 12 *Jyothirlingas* and is the spiritual and cultural centre of the Rameshwaram area. The *Shiva Linga* was established in the temple during the *Treta Yuga* (2nd of the 4 *Yugas*) and has been referenced in several Hindu epics and the temple itself was built in the 12th century.

The legend behind the Rameshwaram temple is as follows. At the end of the Ramayana war, Lord Rama got the *Brahmana Dosham* for killing a *Brahman* (Ravana) and hence he had to install *Shiva Lingas* at four different places to rid himself of this *Dosha* – Rameshwaram temple (India), Manavari temple (Chilaw, Sri Lanka), Thiruketheeswaram (Mannar, Sri Lanka) and Koneswaram Kovil (Trincomalee, Sri Lanka).

At Rameshwaram, Lord Hanuman was sent to *Kailash* to get a *Shiva Linga* for the puja, but he was delayed and since the auspicious time was close, Sita Devi made one out of sand. When he returned, to placate his anger at using another *Linga,* Lord Rama asked him to remove the sand *Linga* and install the *Kailash Linga,* but try as he might he couldn't do it as Sita Devi's *Bhakti* had strengthened the sand *Linga*. Lord Rama then had the *Kailash Linga* installed near the sand one with the promise that anyone who would visit the temple would worship it first. Following this, Vibheeshana installed a Spatika Linga (Quartz) in the temple.

We woke up at 5 a.m., (well I never did fall asleep to begin with thanks to the mosquitoes), did not take a bath unlike in other temples where you are supposed to take a bath before entering, and were at the temple by 5:30 a.m. The puja procedure in Rameshwaram starts by worshipping the *Spatika Linga* between 5 a.m. and 6 a.m. (*Mani Darshanam*). Since the *Spatika Linga* is transparent, the only way to *see* it is by having a light source located behind it (case in point the *diyas* in the temple).

After this, we went to the *Agniteertham* (the Sea next to the temple), the first of the *Teerthas*, had a dip in a placid sea and headed back to the temple to continue the *Teertha Snanam* in the remaining 22 *Teerthas* within the complex. We chose the faster way of doing this by hiring a person to pour the water over us, from these *Teerthas*, instead of waiting in the free queue, where there was a long wait time. (Yes, the fire tailed foxes sold us out.) Each of the *Teerthas* was supposed to grant us various benefits like soul cleansing, longevity, debt removal, absolving of sins etc. In addition, the water drawn from these *Teerthas* was said to have medicinal properties and could cure a variety of diseases.

We changed into dry clothes and went back into the temple for the puja. The special darshan cost us fifty bucks and we got to sit in front of the *Linga* for around five minutes, as opposed to the free *darshan*, where we could have just about caught a glimpse of it. The entire process took us around five hours.

The visit to Ramanathaswamy temple was completely different from any other temple experience and was much more interesting than any other we had been to so far. After the temple visit, we caught a taxi and visited a bunch of places around Rameshwaram like *Ramar Padam, Sita, Lakshmana and Hanuman Teerthas, Saatchi Hanuman temple, Panchamukhi Hanuman temple, Devipattnam, Uttarakosa, and Tirupullani.*

In Tirupullani, we visited a temple of Goddess Mahalakshmi, where people pray for marriage or for children. As soon as they heard this, my parents got excited and got me to perform the puja. I was now supposed to get married within forty-five days. Sheesh. If only it was as easy as doing a puja. If this works, I swear people are going to be queuing up here.

We headed back to Madurai and by the time we had dinner and crashed, it was nearly 1 a.m. We were given strict instructions to wake up and be ready by 5 a.m., to visit the Meenakshi temple. I began to think that walking forty kilometres a day was easier than this boot camp style excursion with my parents!

Day 39: If wishes were fishes, we'd all cast nets

Location: Madurai, Tamil Nadu

We were woken up rather rudely at 5 a.m. and forced to get ready by 5:30 a.m. This sure as hell wasn't fun anymore. As expected, the Madurai Meenakshi Amman temple was magnificent. For additional details, please refer to a *Lonely Planet* or a *Rough Guide*. We were all simply too tired to take note of anything or even take in the experience completely. I had no idea how my family had the energy; maybe the trip had taken its toll on us after all. We went through the motions during the puja ceremony and once it was done, we headed out.

After that, we visited the Thiruparankundram temple and the Koodal Azhagar temple and after performing around three hundred different pujas, we were done for the day. All we wanted to do was get back to the hotel and crash but that wasn't going to be easy.

We hailed an auto and it was just our luck that, the driver turned out to be heavily drunk. We didn't realise this, until he almost drove straight into a truck on the wrong side of the road. We asked him to stop the auto before we crashed, but he refused and instead started to taunt us. My brother somehow managed to get him to stop the auto at which point the goon decided he wanted to fight, pulled out a bottle, and threatened to smash it over my brother's head. My father's paternal instincts kicked in and without saying a word, he stepped up and punched the auto driver in the ear. This disoriented him enough for me to be able to disarm him. Realising that he was in a bad spot, he backed off and fled, but not before he threatened to kill us.

A huge crowd that gathered around us thoroughly enjoyed the scene, none of whom even bothered to help us out. At the end of it, one particular douche bag actually had the gall to come up to us and say that we seemed to be a respectable family, but we were fighting on the streets. What the hell had the world come to? One step forward, two steps backwards seemed to be the case for me.

Anjana Parvatha, the birthplace of Hanuman

Namakkal Anjaneyar

Typical path that we walked on

:oad to Kodai

The temple where we met the old man - déjà vu

Floating stone of Rama Setu

Chariot at Naliappar temple

ɅIahendragiri in all of its glory

The goats that took over our overnight campsite

The Baja 250

Jetewanarama Dagoba

Koneswaram Temple

Lion's Paws at Sigiriya

Road to Wilpattu

The Guide Dog

“Why do you want to buy them?” she asked

PART – 4: Courage

"Courage is being scared to death, but saddling up anyway."

— John Wayne

Days 40 to 41: Get to da Choppa

Location: Madurai, Tamil Nadu

My parents headed out to visit yet another temple, while we decided to relax and read our books. After visiting well over fifty temples in the last few days, it had been a massive overload especially since each visit felt so rushed. Rushing was inevitable, since my parents only had a few days to visit all the temples they had heard so much about. Whatever be the case, we were definitely looking forward to a slower pace of exploration.

At the time of departure, my parents did the usual *rona dhona* scene, asked me to be careful, and call them every day. Their visit had helped us in several ways. Firstly, we now looked forward to the walk more than ever; being made to visit temple after temple made us crave for new and exciting experiences. Secondly, we sent all of the extra stuff – food, clothes and even the bivy back with them. We had concluded that we didn't need any of the food that we were carrying since we could get everything we possibly wanted in any of the towns. Other than the clothes on my back, all I had in the bag was a shirt, a rain jacket, the GPS, ropes, knife, a few Snickers bars, and the bear spray.

"The things you own end up owning you. It's only after you lose everything that you're free to do anything." - Chuck Palahniuk, Fight Club

It was true. As we carried less stuff, we started to relax more. Since we had nothing to lose, we lowered our defences and lost the defensive walls we had built around ourselves. In return, people were friendlier and would go out of their way to help us out. We wondered if we could actually do this once we got back to our regular lives, assuming we got back in one piece.

The next day, we visited the Kasi Viswanatha temple and the Pathira Kaliamman temple in Sivakasi, before making our way back to Sattur and started towards Kovilpatti. We walked along cheerfully, Sri especially so, since he was filled to the brim with the famous Sivakasi Pakoda. As I said before the only thing that ever turned him snarky was an empty stomach. Thanks to the lighter load and mood, we walked faster and soon checked into a hotel.

We opened our maps and started to plot a trail towards Mahendragiri peak. Mahendragiri was definitely going to be touch and go since it was surrounded by thick forest and had several rocky sections. In addition, since we weren't carrying the necessary gear to spend the night, we definitely had to go up and be back down the 1600-metre peak in a single day. There was no question of camping on top without the necessary preparations. With these thoughts running through our heads, we crashed for the night or at least we tried.

"Hey Sam, are you awake?" Sri asked.

"Nope. I am fast asleep."

"I can't sleep."

"Does it look like I care? Hold on for a minute. Let me think."

After a couple of minutes of silence Sri asked, "So?"

"Nope. I still don't care."

"Tell me a story."

"What is wrong with you?"

"Please."

"Ok. There was once a king, who had a naughty horse. The horse wouldn't sleep and would neigh all night. The king sold the horse to a farmer and slept peacefully that night. The end."

"Tell me one with a happy ending."

"The horse neighed that night and the farmer beat it on the head with a stick. The horse died."

"How is that a happy ending?"

"The farmer slept peacefully ever after."

"I wonder why I even bother talking to you."

"You and me both, brother; you and me both."

Day 42: Blank faces, calm as Hindu cows

Location: Kovilpatti, Tamil Nadu

After a quick breakfast, we made short work of the five kilometres from Kovilpatti to the road that led to Kazhugumalai (Kalugmalai). We caught a bus from the junction to the Kalugmalai Asana Murthy temple, an 18th century BCE Murugan temple, located at the base of the Kalugmalai hill. A brief prayer later, we followed the signs to the Jain temple located on the hill past the Murugan temple.

The Jain temple had an image of Bhagawan Parshwanatha, which had been meticulously carved out of the solid rock. There were also several Jain carvings near the temple, which depicted everyday people and their lives. The guide cum guard informed us that the script used for the carvings was 'vatteluttu'. He then led us to the Vettuvan Kovil, a 13th century BCE monolithic temple dedicated to Lord Shiva. The temple had been cut out of the mountain with great precision and the bas-relief carvings near the top of the temple were elaborate. Each side of the temple had a guardian – Brahma, Vishnu, Shiva, Uma Maheswarar carved at the top, and an idol of Lord Ganesha inside. The temple had never been completed and hence was relatively unknown.

As we got back to the highway, dark clouds started to gather and by the time we had walked a couple of kilometres, it started drizzling. The sun kept poking its head out of the clouds every few minutes, ensuring that it was perfect weather for a long walk. We captured some amazing photographs along the way and by 6:30 p.m., were a kilometre from our destination. It was close to dark when all hell broke loose.

We walked past two men, who beckoned me over. They were quite drunk, but we had received plenty of help on this trip from people who were drunk and had no reason to think otherwise, especially after having so many experiences with good and helpful people. We talked for a bit, with them asking me the usual questions of where I was heading, where I was from, and what I was doing. They started talking between themselves for a few minutes and ignored me, so I decided to move on.

I bid them goodbye and started walking towards town. They called me back, but by then I had realised that they were just messing around. I told them politely but firmly that it was getting late and that I was leaving and continued walking. Hearing their raised voices, I felt that there was going to be trouble, so I kept watching them out of the corner of my eye. After I was about twenty feet away, I saw one of them walking towards me. As I turned around to confront him, he caught my backpack, pulled me back, and tried to grab me around my neck.

I had been in this shitty scene before and it had not gone well for me. I ended up with a black eye then, but this time I was better prepared. As soon as he reached for my neck, I twisted around and elbowed him in the face. My elbow caught him right on the nose and most probably broke it. He started bleeding profusely and staggered back in shock. Seeing this, his friend stepped forward, but I already had my knife out. He realised that I wasn't worth the trouble and stayed back.

Sam and Sri were shocked by what was happening. I was shocked as well, but instinct took over and we started running into town. Once in town, we noticed a bus that was heading in the opposite direction and scrambled aboard. We had no intention of getting caught by a mob of his friends later in a hotel. We all knew how scenes like those ended, not too favourably or happily.

As I sat in the bus, I could feel my heart racing thanks to the adrenaline. The entire incident happened in a matter of seconds.

"Did you see how I kicked his ass and saved you both?" Sam asked suddenly, looking to defuse the situation.

"Like hell you did. You were looking to bolt," I replied.

"Why in the hell were you talking to drunken ruffians? They didn't in any way look like decent folk," Sri said.

"Because we decided that we were going to trust people more," I replied.

"That's all fine, but why did you turn your back on them? That was incredibly stupid. They could have done anything – thrown a stone, rushed you, conked you with a bottle, anything. Let's not do that ever again."

"Agreed. Mistake made and lesson learnt."

The bus was headed to Tirunelveli, which we figured would be safe as it was a tourist hub, making us hard to find. We hoped that they didn't see which bus we got on and come after us. Eventually, we got into town and checked into a hotel, right next to the police station. Being careful never hurt anyone.

Sam said that he had expected this to happen and that it was the reason why he had insisted on carrying the knife in the first place. Thanks to the incident, his misanthropy was firmly in place and out in arms. Considering the events of the last few days, I now had serious doubts in people as well. I was back to square one. Sure, the numbers didn't add up, there were dozens of people who had helped us and we had run into assholes twice, but I remained unconvinced. The raw emotion of the event weighed heavily on my mind and smote out any logical appeal.

Days 43 to 44: All animals are equal, but some animals are more equal than others

Location: Tirunelveli, Tamil Nadu

The adrenaline rush from the previous day had left us exhausted us, and we woke up late. We decided to play it safe and not take too many risks, so we went around Tirunelveli and visited the Nellaiappar temple (a twin temple dedicated to Lord Shiva and Goddess Parvathi) and the 'Get well Anjaneyar' temple (a Hanuman temple with a statue nearly 77 feet in height). The priest at the Anjaneyar temple informed us of its uniqueness – the idol was of *Vishwaroopam* Anjaneya and there were only five other temples like these in the world – Namakkal (44 feet), Suchindram (22 feet), Nanganaloor, Chennai (32 feet), Dindigul, Seenalampatti, and Nuwara Eliya (Sri Lanka).

The next day after a few hours of uneventful walking, we ended up in Kalakkad.

Day 45: I now walk into the wild

Location: Kalakkad, Tamil Nadu

The plan for the day was to walk fifteen kilometres along highway 177, after which we would head off towards Mahendragiri and climb it! The road moved in parallel to the range and we looked forward to seeing the mountain first hand. After a few hours of walking, we reached Thirukurungudi, which had a fifteen hundred years old temple of Lord Vishnu. The temple had beautiful statues of Lord Hanuman, Garuda, and Sri Azhagiyanambi with Sridevi and Bhoodevi by his side. As we stepped out of the temple, we noticed that the sky was full of ominous black clouds. We were now in a race against the rain; we had to get to the base of Mahendragiri before the rain hit or risk getting stuck in the middle of nowhere.

We walked at a quick pace for a couple of hours and by 2 p.m., were walking through the fields towards Mahendragiri. Thanks to the heavy cloud cover, we couldn't see much of the mountain or its surroundings. Luckily, we had marked down the coordinates of a temple on the south side of the mountain, where we had planned to camp for the night. From our research, the south face seemed to be the easiest face to ascend. As luck would have it, before we reached the temple, the rain hit us hard. We just about managed to pull out the space blanket and wrap it around ourselves to avoid getting drenched.

The rain let up after an hour, but we had hardly walked five hundred metres before it came thundering down again. We were debating whether to push forward to the temple or look for some shelter nearby, when we noticed an old, abandoned house. It was located about one and a half kilometres from the east face of the mountain. We ran into the building and considered our options – we could camp there for the night and save our energy for the climb or wait for the rain to stop and go about looking for the temple before it got dark. We chose the former.

Eventually, the cloud cover broke and we got our first *real* view of Mahendragiri. It was only then that we realised the magnitude of the task that we faced. Mahendragiri was huge and surrounded by thick forests on all sides. The east side consisted of a three hundred metre sheer rock face, which was nearly impossible to ascend without climbing gear. By contrast, the north and the south faces seemed more approachable. We decided to wait until the morning and then decide on the route for the ascent.

We covered the windows with palm leaves, dragged some thorny bushes to serve as a door, and collected some grass to serve as a mattress. We noticed that the room stank horribly and checked our shoes for shit but that wasn't the case; little did we know that we were about to find out why. It started raining again and suddenly, a herd of goats charged through the *bush door* and straight into the room. A minute later, we were left standing in the room surrounded by goats with not an inch of space to move. The buggers managed to open my backpack and ate most of our food. On top of that, one of them had the gall to piss on my boots.

We stood there awkwardly trying to figure out our next move, when a goatherd walked in and shooed the goats out. We talked to him and learnt that nobody went up Mahendragiri and hence there was no trail. Sri noticed that the goatherd was freezing in the rain and gave him my space blanket; he said that it would serve the goatherd better. He was probably fishing for good karma.

After the goatherd left, we took stock of supplies and realised that our food situation was grim. After the *Mongoat raid*, all we had left was two energy bars, a pack of biscuits and, two litres of water. We tried to get a fire started, but since all of the wood was wet, we were denied that comfort as well. We decided to get up on the roof of the house and deal with the possibility of rain rather than the snakes, centipedes, scorpions, and other creepy crawlies.

Once we were on the roof and had nothing else to do, my fears started to surface. We were headed into a forest, located right next to a tiger reserve; problem is, the tigers did not know the boundaries. Even if we considered that the chances of running into a tiger were negligible, we could still run into bears, elephants, or leopards.

Everybody has fears, some rational, like the fear of heights, snakes, or water; others irrational, like public speaking, change, and sleeping among others. I had a fear of sharks and crocodiles thanks to watching *Jaws* and *Alligator* as a kid. Unfortunately, my dad insisted that I swam regularly and the only time possible for both of us was late in the evening. Swimming in dark pools was petrifying; I would freeze up in fear even at the slightest ripple. I eventually managed to overcome my fears through a coping mechanism – if I found something I was afraid of, I **had to** go ahead and face it. I called upon it then, hoping it would get me through the Mahendragiri nightmare as well.

Sam probably realized that I was terrified, because he started reading out the 'Bene Gesserit' saying from *Dune, "I must not fear. Fear is the mind killer. Fear is the little – death that brings total obliteration. I will face my fear. I will permit it to pass over me and through me…"*

"…and when it has gone past I will turn the inner eye to see its path. Where the fear has gone there will be nothing. Only I will remain," I said, completing the saying.

It did not help much, but I knew what had to be done and there was no backing out now.

Day 46: SNAFU

Location: Whereabouts unknown

I now knew what 'Tom' must have felt like at the end of an episode of 'Tom and Jerry'; every bone and muscle in my body hurt. My hands were so badly scratched that I couldn't touch anything without pain shooting up my arms. Severe dehydration had ensured that my stomach had shut down completely and my throat was so parched that it hurt when I swallowed. To top things off, one of my ribs hurt like it was broken, probably from the fall. My buddies, Sam and Sri weren't doing all too well either.

We started off well enough, attempting a hard but doable day ascent and descent of Mount Mahendragiri in Nagercoil. Somewhere down the line though, we lost both our strength and our will. Now, all we wanted to do was get out alive. So, what happened that day?

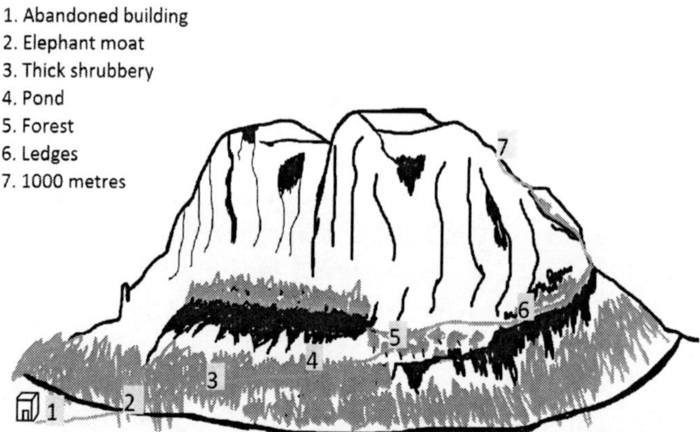

At 6 a.m., we found ourselves staring at Mahendragiri, trying to identify the most optimal path for the ascent. You know you are in trouble when you aren't even sure about the route to take on a trek. We had two choices - follow our original plan and climb the south face or walk across the ridge on the east face and climb the north face. We called some experienced trekkers back home to seek their advice, but the cell reception was bad and we could only catch bits and pieces of the conversation. From whatever little we heard, we thought they were trying to tell us to climb the south face.

Since we weren't sure of what they said or how the ascent would be from the south side, we chose to go with our gut instinct, which insisted on the north side. That was the first of a series of mistakes, which would cost us dearly. While following your instincts is good, a good plan and sound advice is usually a better option.

By 6:30 a.m., we were walking towards the east face of the mountain. Between the base of the mountain and us, lay one and a half kilometres of thorny scrub forest. As we reached the edge of the scrubs, we ran across an elephant moat, which we jumped over easily. The scrub was so thick that we could barely see a couple of feet ahead of us; if we ran into any animal in the scrubs, it would be trouble. We found a game trail and followed it for a while, until it started branching away from the mountain. We stepped off the trail and headed towards the mountain, crawling through the scrubs as they got thicker, and eventually below the scrubs. The thorns tore into our clothes and skin, but we managed to get them off easily by pushing back instead of pulling forward against them.

As if that wasn't painful enough, the safety cap of the bear repellent pepper spray fell off and it started spraying wildly. My eyes burned, but we didn't have much water to spare and since we couldn't leave it in the middle of nowhere, I taped it up thus rendering it effectively useless. Just brilliant! The only safety backup we had in case of an animal attack was out of commission.

We continued crawling through the thorns and after an hour, were at the base of the mountain. Along the way, we managed to spook at least half a dozen Sambar deer. There have been several reported cases of them goring people to death with their antlers. Mercifully, they ran away as soon as they spotted us. We were thankful that it was just deer and not elephants or bears.

At the base of the mountain, we stumbled upon a small pond where elephants drank water and pooped in. We wondered what the elephant must have been thinking – *"Damn I'm thirsty. Ooh, there's some water. But wait; let me poop in it first to add vitamins, amino acids, minerals so that my calf and I grow stronger, faster, and smarter."* We washed up, filtered, and drank water and I carried two litres with me hoping it would suffice. This was probably the worst of our mistakes. Once the sun warmed up, the water went out of us like piss from a puppy – fervently and frequently.

We found another game trail and followed it until we ran into a dried up stream, which seemed to lead all the way up the mountain. Following the stream saved us from the thorns, but granted its own share of problems – steep rock faces that tested our non-existent rock-climbing skills and wore us out, slowly, but surely. Progress up the mountain was slow and we kept losing water, energy, and time. Despite adding ORS to the water and drinking it frequently, we were rapidly dehydrating and getting weaker. We took several breaks and saw a variety of birds and monkeys (Rhesus and lion-tailed macaques) that got our spirits up.

Time flew by and at 11 a.m., forget about being close to the summit, we hadn't even reached the north face. We pushed ourselves to move faster and after another hour came across a sheer rock face, which seemed impossible to climb without professional rock climbing gear. We had somehow veered off course and ended up on the wrong side of the sheer face. We now had another choice, either backtrack all the way down and climb up the right way or climb across the face. We stupidly chose to climb across the rock face, simple because we did not have the energy or the time to backtrack and find our way around the rock face.

We studied the rock face and found that it had a few crevices and rocky holds that we could use to cross. The problem was the footholds or the lack of them; they were far and few. This meant that we had to rely on our upper body strength to hang onto the holds and get across. Not very worrisome considering that our shoulders were in decent shape, thanks to the heavy backpacks that we had been lugging around for the last few weeks. I took the lead and went across checking the strength of the holds and for loose rocks. At one point, I made the mistake of transferring my weight to a hold, before checking if it would take my weight. Big mistake. As soon as I put some weight on it, the rock came loose. Luckily, I had maintained a strong grip with my other hand, which saved me from a twenty-metre fall. A fall there would have been disastrous, as nobody knew our exact position and rescue wouldn't have made it in time.

Eventually, we got across the rock face and reached a section of forest that grew around the mountain. While it was shady, it was quite steep and we had to drag ourselves up, using our arms to hold onto the trees. My legs had given way due to the lactic acid build up and metres now seemed like kilometres. I was running on fumes and prayed to Lord Hanuman to give me the strength to go on. In hindsight, that was probably the only thing that kept me going forward. We were all tired to the point of exhaustion, but kept pushing onward without a word.

By 2 p.m., we were still around eight hundred metres from the top. This was where the forest cleared and we finally caught a view of the area surrounding the mountain including the dam. We had run out of food and water a couple of hours ago and were severely dehydrated. Thanks to that and the strenuous climbing, we were completely exhausted and each step was a herculean effort. Yet, we were not ready to give up.

We took some pictures and collected our energy for one last push. The final stretch to the summit was very steep and required us to rock climb, so I left my pack behind and started the ascent. It was hard work with the sun blazing down on us. I knew that I was taking a huge risk by climbing in such a dehydrated state, but I couldn't just give up without giving it a shot. I managed to climb a mere fifty-metres, before a wave of dizziness hit me. I realized there was no strength left in my body. We all felt the same, but no one said a word. The truth was a harsh whip, which none of us had the heart to wield and so we sat in silence. I rested, prayed, and then pushed on; I told myself that I wasn't going to wimp out like I did. Another fifty metres, rinse and repeat.

By 3 p.m., we had only managed to climb to a height of one thousand metres; we were still six hundred metres from the top. As I started crawling again, another wave of dizziness hit me. I felt a strong urge to throw up, even though my stomach was completely empty, and I almost blacked out. If there was one thing that past trekking experience had taught me, it's that one should always have an established cut off time; a time after which the chances of returning safely go down exponentially. This was our cut off time. Before starting on the ascent, we had decided that we would start heading back at 3 p.m., whether we made it to the top or not. We all knew this and yet nobody said a word as I continued climbing. Ten minutes later, I reached a spot where I couldn't find any holds to reach up to. I doubled back to find another route, but that ended in the same manner. I panicked, then calmed down and checked again, but there was no way up. This was it. End of the line.

We could see the top - enticing, calling, and mocking us. The realisation that we had failed hit me and I felt like shit. We had never considered the possibility that we would fail to reach the top. Failing hadn't even been an option. We had vastly underestimated the time and effort required to make the ascent and set ourselves up to fail. We discussed the option of camping there overnight and taking a shot at the summit the next morning, but we all knew that it was a horrible idea. We did not have the gear to spend the night on the steep slopes and we didn't have any food or water either. Being stupid and making mistakes was one thing, being suicidal was another thing. We convinced ourselves that we could always come back for another attempt.

Having accepted our failure, we decided to head back. Our biggest challenge lay in making the descent to the base and getting out of the forest before sunset. It was already a little past 3 p.m., so we had about three hours of daylight left. It seemed like an impossible task, considering that we had no idea of the route we had taken on our way up.

That was the lowest point for me. The doubt that I had overcome earlier now burst forth with renewed vigour. He had been waiting for this opportunity ever since we had met the old man in the temple, *"Let's look at everything you have accomplished on this trip. Wait…why is this list empty? Let me tell you why. It's because you accomplished NOTHING. You failed in everything you set out to do. You wanted to walk the entire way, but failed to do that. You tried to silence me, but failed. You set out to get your faith back and failed at that as well, quite spectacularly, may I add. You couldn't even finish a simple task like getting up this mountain, despite all the help you got along the way. Do you remember what I told you? That you misread a dream and took it too far. Did you listen? NOPE."*

"But the dream was real. The old man is proof of that," I said, trying to fight back.

"Oh, is that so. Ok, let us assume that you didn't misread the dream. Even if that was the case, you still didn't do what you were supposed to do. You cheated by catching buses and accepting rides when you were supposed to walk the entire way. This is your punishment for cheating and for being stupid."

I had no answers to what he said.

"Don't worry, there is a silver lining to all of this. There is one thing that you have accomplished – you have succeeded in getting yourself and your friends killed. They will pay with their lives for your stupidity and desperation in following your dream blindly. You have no food or water, it's close to darkness, and the animals of the wild will soon be out hunting for food. There is no escaping this and you know it."

I sat there in silence, listening to his venom.

He wasn't done though, "*Now, listen to me, at least this one time. I have a solution to all of your problems. Why don't you just sit down and enjoy the beautiful view. Just relax and let go for a few hours and it will all be over. You will get all your answers. You don't have to struggle, you can let it end in peace. What are you going to accomplish anyway by going back.*"

At this point, when I was wallowing in self-pity and considering giving up, Sri pointed out something to me. Sam had built a cairn and was praying with a serene expression on his face. The guy never prayed; even in temples he just looked at the architecture and wandered about, while Sri and I prayed. We looked at him in astonishment and he said that he had offered his apologies for not making it to the top, after promising to do so. He said that God understood and would watch over us, as we made our way down. Sam told me that he had always believed in my dream and now it was time for me to believe in him.

The doubt in my head tried to counter, "*There is no way what he is saying is true. God doesn't talk to anyone. He is lying to you; betraying you. There is no point in fighting this. Why struggle at your end? Just sit here and relax; at least it won't be a struggle.*"

It was a delicious thought, considering how tired I was, but Sam and Sri were never going to let that happen. They kept pushing me to get up and move. Finally, I did get up, if only to escape their incessant nagging. I ignored doubt, picked up my gear and staggered downhill. Nobody had a plan. We walked through the thick forest in the general direction of the highway, not even bothering to look for a trail. It was easier walking downhill and for the most part, momentum was what kept us going. Thanks to the dehydration, we experienced raw thirst for the first time. At one point, we stopped next to a rock, which had a drop of water trickling down every five seconds and licked it for thirty minutes to sate our thirst. Sometime later, we found a pool of murky water with leaves, mud, and a decomposing prawn; what we did there is all but obvious.

After a little while, I was completely worn out and couldn't even walk straight. I started using a trick I picked up from *Bear Grylss*, sitting down and sliding with one leg straight out and the other leg folded to function as a brake. This worked quite well and I covered a fair bit of ground using this technique. At one point, when I was sliding downhill at a rapid pace, I had a premonition of sorts – a voice warned me to stop. I reacted immediately and managed to grab hold of a creeper, barely managing to stop myself from tumbling over the edge of a cliff. I thought it was either Sri or Sam who warned me, but they hadn't noticed the cliff either. Was there someone else around or was Lord Hanuman actually watching over us?

At another point, we had to rappel down a thirty-foot drop to reach the forest floor. Luckily, we were still carrying the parachute cord. As I was rappelling down, the voice called out again, "Careful. Look up." As I did, I heard the sound of a large rock crashing through the vegetation. I couldn't tell where the rock was headed and just swung hard to my left instinctively. A fraction of a second later, a large rock flew inches past my face and crashed onto the floor below. There was definitely a voice there, saving our asses.

We continued downhill, using every trick in the book to conserve whatever energy remained and get out before nightfall – jump, run, slide, rappel, and crawl. Ants, centipedes, and other insects crawled all over my body, biting down hard (I must have hit a nest somewhere), but I was too tired to react to the pain. I stumbled through thorns without bothering to step away as they tore into my skin; I was...we were beyond caring. I heard the voice one last time, just before I stumbled into a clearing in the jungle and then it was gone.

At 6 p.m., we were still in the forest, but luckily found a game trail and followed it until we hit the scrub forest. It was now dark and we had a kilometre of scrub to crawl under to get to civilization. We were afraid of running into any snakes or scorpions, but were left with no other choice, than to push forward under the light of the headlamp. We somehow managed to make it through the scrubs, without any incident.

The only thing left now was the long crawl back to civilization. While gathering our energies and saying our prayers, we took one last look at our nemesis and promised ourselves that we would be back. It took us an hour to drag ourselves to a farm that was barely a kilometre away. The farmer was shocked at our condition, yet was kind enough to give us a bucket of water. We were extremely thirsty, but knew that drinking too much water could lead to water intoxication, so we had to hold back on the water. Once we reached the highway, a kind trucker took pity on our condition and gave us a ride into town.

We had gone through a myriad range of emotions – hopefulness, happiness, *adrenaline,* sadness, anger, bitterness, disgust, and hope. Despite making several mistakes and grossly underestimating the trek, we had survived thanks to the warnings from Lord Hanuman. It is said that faith is renewed in troubling times and in our case, this proved to be true. There wasn't a shade of doubt what I believed then. I believed with all my heart that Lord Hanuman had been watching over us.

We went to a hotel in Nagercoil and were informed that it was full; the same thing happened with a few other hotels, until I caught a glimpse of myself in a mirror at one of the hotels and understood the problem. We looked like shit – covered from head to toe in mud, dirt, and blood, torn clothes, cuts on our hands, feet and face that were bleeding, leaves, and cobwebs all over our hair and backpacks. The hotel staff must have thought we were beggars or lunatics and refused us rooms. We eventually managed to get a room by showing my passport to the front desk manager.

Day 47: The cake is a lie

Location: Nagercoil, Tamil Nadu

I woke up at 8 a.m., and no matter how much I tried, I couldn't fall asleep again. Old habits die hard. My body hurt in places that I didn't know existed and despite taking a painkiller the pain didn't ease up one bit. Eventually, we headed out to buy books and clothes. My pants were completely shredded from the Mahendragiri debacle and my shirt was faded thanks to the weeks of relentless sun, beating down on it.

In addition, we had lost a lot of weight in the last few weeks and my waist size had gone down from thirty-two inches to twenty-eight inches. It was something I hadn't noticed until then, probably because it was a gradual change. A quick glance in the mirror showed what I looked like – a stick insect wearing oversized pants.

We picked up whatever we liked, packed up, and moved to Kanyakumari. All along the way, Sam had been unusually quiet and we were about to find out why.

"Did you even notice that I'm pissed at you?" he burst out abruptly.

"How could I miss it? I was enjoying the silence," I replied.

"You almost got us killed, you frickin German polar bear."

"Well, we are alive. So what's your complaint?"

"Nothing. What's the status?"

"I don't think there is any doubt left in my mind," I replied.

"What about you Sam?" Sri asked.

"What about me? I got you out alive didn't I? What more do you want?"

"The truth. What happened when you built the cairn?"

"Nothing. I offered my prayers and I *knew* we would be ok. I can't explain why, but I just knew and that's what I told you."

"I clearly heard the voice that warned me several times on the way down the mountain. I know what to believe now," I said.

"What did it sound like?"

"It was a male voice and was soft but clear. Something about it made me pay complete attention. That was probably the reason why I could react so quickly to the warnings. Oddly, I can't think of anyone's voice that I know of to compare it to."

"You know what you heard, right?"

"Yes. I do."

"Ok. I guess you finally have your faith back. So, what now? Are we done with the trip? Are we heading back?" Sri asked.

"Well, we have come so far and I have my faith back, but I am curious as to what else is in store for us, so we might as well head to Sri Lanka as planned and see what happens."

"Well, that was easy and quite an anti-climax."

"No it wasn't. We almost died on that mountain," Sam said.

"And yet I don't hear your usual snarky self," I replied.

"It's because I got something out of that as well. Nothing more, nothing less."

"Do you remember when I told you that one day you would believe as well? What do you have to say now?"

"You had to say 'I told you so', didn't you. You pompous fuck."

I had passed way over my *tipping point,* on the way down the mountain and come to the realisation that what we had experienced were signs and not just coincidences. The voice wasn't my imagination or my instinct, I **had** heard it, and I was now sure of my faith. Even though my body hurt, reclaiming my faith made me feel better than I had felt in days. I still wanted to go to Sri Lanka, as it was part of our original plan. I was curious to see where that journey would lead to, now that I had my faith back. I wondered what Lord Hanuman had in store for us.

Days 48 to 52: If strength is justice, then is powerlessness a crime?

Location: Kanyakumari, Tamil Nadu

We were all quite happy to be done with the walking. All we wanted to do was eat and sleep, but we still had to see Kanyakumari since we were there. Squirrel mode priorities! Over the next few days, we visited tourist spots in and around Kanyakumari like Sunrise point, Vivekananda Memorial, Thiruvalluvar statue, Kanyakumari Temple, the Triveni Sangam, Vattakottai fort (circular fort), the Nataraja temple, and the Suchindram Anjaneyar temple.

The last tourist spot that we planned to see was Sunset point. It was a breath-taking sight and the sun seemed to acknowledge the hordes of eager visitors, with a vibrant display of orange, yellow, blue, and violets as it set.

"That was amazing. Wonder what it would be like to sail off into the sunset?" Sri wondered aloud.

"Well for starters, the ship would be filled to the brim with *desis* staring at the *goras* and you would hear people shouting, 'Chai biscuit, sasta maal chahiye, butter chicken paneer butter' loudly until no directions could be heard and the ship crashed straight into the big island over there," Sam replied.

"Everybody would swim to the island in silence, until some brilliant hero comes up with 'chai salt biscuit' or 'cheap tickut on lifeboat to India, only phive rupees'. Then everybody blames the *goras* for incompetent ship navigation behind their backs, blame the Gods for their misfortune and proceed to kiss every one of the goras asses with great enthusiasm. After that..."

"Ok. We get it, you xenophobic mongrel," Sri replied.

"I'm not xenophobic. I just hate suck ups."

We contacted a travel agent, who informed us that tickets for the ferry were available at Thoothukudi. After we visited the tourist spots in Kanyakumari, we headed over and picked up the tickets. It was then that we realised that we had a major problem on our hands – my passport, which I had been carrying in a waterproof arm pouch had somehow gotten drenched during our misadventure at Mahendragiri. The protective film had peeled off partially leaving it looking oddly suspicious. As if I did not look suspicious enough already with cuts and bruises all over my body.

After a huge argument, which as usual led to nowhere, we decided to leave it in the hands of Lord Hanuman and the Sri Lankan immigrations officials, to decide if we would go ahead or go home. It was a depressing thought – going back home in this manner after making it so far, but we had no say in the matter.

We headed out and picked up some Cashew *Macaroon* – a sugary sweet specialty of Thoothukudi. On our way back to the hotel, we ran into a huge procession with a band, chariots, elephants, horses, and what looked like the entire town.

Thanks to his sugar rush, Sri immediately got excited, "Cool! Look at the elephant that's all dressed up. Let's take a picture with it."

Sam wasn't too happy at the sight of a captive elephant and declined, "I'm quite happy staying here."

Suddenly, some idiot decided that lighting fireworks right in front of the elephant was a logically appropriate thing to do. As expected, the poor elephant promptly panicked and the situation turned a little dicey. Thankfully, the mahout handled the situation quite well and calmed the poor animal down.

"Who in his right mind would light a firecracker in front of an elephant?" No wonder we hear reports of elephants running amok in processions in the south," Sam said.

"If I was the elephant, I would have shoved the cracker up his ass, punched him in the face, and for good measure sat on him."

We watched as the procession snaked away through town and hoped there wouldn't be any untoward incidents. After what we just witnessed, it wouldn't be surprising to learn otherwise.

"Only two things are infinite, the universe, and human stupidity, and I'm not sure about the former." - Albert Einstein.

Day 53: Borders I have never seen one. But I have heard they exist in the minds of some people

Location: Thoothukudi, Tamil Nadu

Over the last few days, we had spent a lot of time looking up locations of sites related to Lord Hanuman and the Ramayana in Sri Lanka and had marked out the various places we needed to visit. The sites were spread across Sri Lanka and many of them were located in remote locations. Considering the amount of time we had and the fact that we were pretty drained from the walk, we decided to stick to our original plan of exploring Sri Lanka on motorcycles.

Satisfied with our brilliant planning and with congratulations all around, we headed to the harbour to board the ferry. This was where we met Xin and Chun. They were from China and had been travelling for the last fifty days through Tibet, Nepal, and India. We talked about our plans or at least Sam, Sri, and I did. We thought we had been shallow in our planning but Xin and Chun took the cake. They had absolutely no knowledge of Sri Lanka and were completely dependent on their 'Lonely Planet' for information.

You would figure that this was a sure fire way to get suckered and have a horrible trip, but that was not the case. In the fifty days that they had travelled so far, they said they had not even had one bad experience. That was impossible, heck we were Indians and we had a few bad experiences on our trip. Maybe it was their perspective; maybe they somehow took every experience in a positive frame of mind. Whatever it was, it was working and they seemed to having the time of their lives.

What they told us next was even more incredible; they had spent Rs. 40000 so far on the trip and for twenty days in India, they had spent only Rs. 20000. This was inclusive of food, travel, sightseeing, and accommodation expenses. Travelling on 500 rupees a day per person was insane; we knew the language and yet we were spending close to 1500 rupees. We wondered how they were able to manage this incredible feat. We would get our answer very soon.

We passed through immigrations and boarded the ferry. Soon, a tug appeared and towed the ship out of the harbour. After a couple of hours, dinner was served and that's when the shit hit the fan or in this case, the puke did.

"Look at all these people puking their guts out! It's like those scenes in the movies, where the hero's sister and wife both get pregnant and the news has to be broken to the audience," Sam exclaimed.

"I think I'm going to be sick looking at them puke," Sri said.

"Here, let me help. Imagine them crapping in addition to the puking," Sam replied.

"Most people can manage the left-right motion; it's the up-down motion from the wave action that gets them. Try lying down, it should help."

We hit a big wave and the food in our stomach went around like clothes in a washing machine. "That was a good one. Now watch closely as half the people try desperately to hold the food down," Sam said chuckling. He was clearly enjoying this.

"There's the crew to the rescue. They are handing out anti-nausea pills. Hooray!" Sri exclaimed.

A few minutes were all it took for his happiness to disappear. "Hooray!" Sam said, mimicking Sri's exclamation, "They are throwing up the pills as well! This party ain't ending so easily!"

Sri finally gave up, "Let's just go, and crash. I have had enough of watching people puke. We can wake up in the morning and watch dolphins off the bow."

PART – 5: Strength

"Strength does not come from physical capacity. It comes from an indomitable will."

— Mahatma Gandhi

Day 54: Time flies like an arrow; fruit flies like a banana

Location: Colombo, Sri Lanka

Welcome to Sri Lanka – land of the funky haircuts, wicked traffic, and smiley faces! We docked at 8 a.m., and were herded towards immigration so slowly, that we thought we would die of old age by the time we got into Colombo. Our worries regarding the condition of my passport turned out to be meaningless though. The friendly officer, without a second thought, gave me a Sri Lankan visa.

My life has been full of terrible misfortunes most of which never happened – Michel de Montaigne.

We ran into a scam artist even before we stepped out of the harbour. A guy walked up to Chun and told her that Indian rupees couldn't be exchanged in banks or foreign exchange counters in Sri Lanka. The *Good Samaritan* offered to illegally exchange the money himself at a rate of 2.2 SLR per INR as opposed to the actual exchange rate of 2.4-2.5 SLR. Sam sensed that there was something off about the guy and warned us – he seemed too eager to please, which was always a dead ringer for a scam artist.

We warned Xin and Chun and asked them not to exchange all of their money, but they panicked and did exactly that; they exchanged 40000 INR and ended up losing ~8000 INR in the process. We on the other hand exchanged just enough to get around for a day. The funny part was that once they found out about their loss, they regretted it for a grand total of five minutes. This was probably why they said that they had no bad experiences on their trip – their happy go lucky attitude.

We headed towards Mount Lavinia for cheap accommodation, as hotels close to the centre of Colombo were expensive. Once there, we found out first-hand how the couple managed to travel so cheap. While we were okay with rooms charging us 1500 – 2000 SLR, the couple would have none of it. They insisted that it was too expensive and that we would find a cheaper option. Three hours, six kilometres of walking and thirty hotels later, we arrived at a *love hotel*, where the 'manager' quoted a price of 500 SLR for two hours. The couple insisted that they wanted it for the entire night, while the manager assured them that they wouldn't need it for so long. We watched in amazement wondering if they were oblivious to the fact that it was a *love hotel*, or whether they really didn't care as long as it was cheap. We decided it would be impolite to butt in and waited patiently as they negotiated the price down to 1600 SLR for two rooms. This was their secret – a near perfect cocktail of patience, persistence, and bull headedness. Since we planned to get out of Colombo the next day, we weren't particularly bothered about where we were going to stay for the night.

Later in the evening, we visited the Panchamukha Anjaneyar temple in Kalubowila. It was a small temple with a beautiful idol of Lord Hanuman in his Panchamukha form. We had heard that riding motorcycles in Sri Lanka was pretty much a suicidal affair, so we prayed to Lord Hanuman for a safe journey.

We headed back to Mount Lavinia, where we found that a huge fair had been setup. It brought back a flood of good memories from our school days and of one eventful experience from a trip to Sikkim. We were trekking through a remote area of Sikkim and at the end of the day went to see a village fair. The locals invited us into one of the stalls, served some of the local delicacies, and then we had this gem of a conversation:

"Do you see that guy jumping up and down and dancing maniacally?" the stranger sitting next to me, asked conspiratorially.

"Yeah. What about him?" I replied.

"He is an alcoholic."

"No shit, really? I couldn't tell."

"He is also the local Superintendent of Police."

"How would you know?"

"I'm his assistant, and guess what?" he asked, as he rubbed his hands gleefully.

"What?" I asked, taking the bait.

"He will make the lot of you dance soon!"

True to the constable's words, a few drinks later, the SP made sure that all of us were *having fun* and dancing awkwardly. The performance culminated with every one of us having to perform our regional versions of dances much to the amusement of everyone present. In all honesty, it was a lot of fun and the next morning as we walked out of town we received plenty of waves and thumbs ups for our performance. It was a story for a lifetime.

We expected something on those lines as we walked into the fair. Ideally, the sign that read, "Free entry for children below 6," should have served as fair warning, but the memory had made us warm and fuzzy and we charged in without a second thought. Turned out that it was a school fair; you know the ones packed to the brim with loud and annoying brats. We managed to stay for a grand total of twenty minutes before we felt suicidal and bailed to the beach, which was very much alive since it was a Saturday night. Unfortunately, we were exhausted to the point that five minutes into a conversation, I nearly dozed off. I decided to call it a night, had dinner, and headed back to the hotel. As the wise sensei Roger Murtaugh, said – *"I'm too old for this shit!"*

Day 55: It's time to kick ass and chew bubble gum... and I'm all outta gum.

Location: Still in Colombo, Sri Lanka

Since Xin and Chun were not interested in a motorcycle trip, we said our goodbyes and headed out to pick up our wheels. I believe that when the Fugees sang 'Killing me softly', they must have been referring to *Tuk Tuk* drivers in Sri Lanka. They pose next to the Tuk Tuks with innocent smiles, but as soon as you get in, they transform into the *Ghost Rider* and drive like maniacs.

Take your eyes off the road for a second and be prepared to get a concussion from your head hitting the *safety* rod as they brake and swerve. If you think you are safe on the outside, think again. The only difference being on the outside is that you get to see their crazy infectious smile, as they run you over. The best in India would probably pale in comparison to these demonic drivers.

Thanks to our protection prayers from the previous day, we managed to reach the office of the 'Colombo Rentals' without any loss of life or limb albeit with wet pants. We talked to the owner and the deal we got there was – 17000 SLR for 17 days for a *Hero Honda Hunk* or 20000 SLR for a *Yamaha*, roughly $9 per day. The price of $9, even in the off-season was quite cheap. However, he was willing to give us the motorcycles only two days later with the added clause that we needed to hold valid Sri Lankan driver's licenses. We called up 'Sha Lanka' and got an offer of – $18 per day for a Honda *Baja* or $15 for a *Hunk*, but he was closed for the day.

With nothing else to do for the day, we headed back to Mount Lavinia and moved to a hotel that was closer to the beach. We spent the afternoon finalising the route for our motorcycle ride.

Later that evening we went to the beach and ran into a couple of lifeguards. We started talking and they told us about the life saving scene in Sri Lanka and how bad the off-season was for them. Sam warned us that there was a scam coming and sure enough, it was there. One of the life guards told us a sob story about his wife and kids that could have given Bollywood a run for its money. We could see it plain and simple that he was trying to swindle us, but Sri still ended up giving him some money much to the chagrin of Sam and myself. We didn't say anything right away, but once we reached the hotel all hell broke loose.

"Couldn't you see that he was scamming you?" I asked.

"I knew that he was scamming me, but it was only because he needed the money. Lifeguards in the sub-continent, for all their hard work, are paid peanuts. It's not glamorous like *Baywatch*," Sri replied.

"You, my friend, are a daft moron," was Sam's reply, "I can't believe you actually managed to beat a million other sperm."

"His brain is on permanent power saving mode," I added.

"We did make a couple of new friends," Sri said, trying to show us the silver lining.

"More like your kidneys and other transferable organs made friends," Sam replied.

"You need to trust people more. You know how much help we received from absolute strangers all through our trip. What more do you need to believe in people?"

"Oh come on. We all know how people are. They are selfish, greedy, and will do anything to get themselves ahead. All of us have experienced these assholes first hand. Do I need a better reason?"

"Let me make a logical appeal. How many people that you know are complete assholes? I mean absolute assholes with zero morals, not people who are good at times and evil at other times. Give me a percentage."

"Complete? Hmm, maybe five per cent give or take a few."

"Similar to what we experienced on the trip. Logically, you would discount them as anomalies and look at all the good the others do."

"It's because the evil these assholes do outweighs all the good that the rest of the people do. Weighted averages, yeah."

"So all the acts of kindness, loyalty, love, and selflessness performed by the other ninety-five per cent serve no purpose?"

"Pretty much."

"I know you don't actually believe that for a second, so stop bullshitting and tell us the actual reason."

"Why would I not believe that?"

"Because if you did, you would never give any money to charity. You would only do that if you believe people are capable of being good."

"So let's try this again? What's the reason?"

"Fine, the reason I do not trust people or depend on them is because when they fail or let me down, it hurts. For example, how you guys messed up the Mahendragiri climb."

"And your solution is to stop believing in people?"

"Yup. Why go through the hassle of having expectations and feeling miserable when people don't live up to them anyway. Isn't that what the Gita says as well? Do you duty, don't expect anything?"

"That's only true if you are sincere about it, not when you are cynical and jaded. That's poison and it will slowly corrupt you and in turn us."

"Hmph," was his response, as he shrugged his shoulders dismissively.

"Let's try something out. Until the end of the trip, we will put our trust in people completely. We will believe with open hearts come what may and at the end, we will see if we come out better for it."

"Let me get this right. What you are suggesting is that we spend the next few weeks looking for humanity in a country with decades of civil war, where people have done the worst possible things to each other. Count me in. I know what the outcome will be anyway and I'm willing to get us screwed over to prove my point."

"What about you, hero?"

"Do I have a choice? It's either this or a lifetime of mistrust and cloak and dagger games?" I replied.

We were all in agreement with Sri's weird idea. What was the worst that could happen anyway? We could die or get seriously injured. No biggie. On the other hand, if the idea were to succeed, the reward would be worth it.

The lifeguard called us later that night and offered to take us to a temple in his hometown. Maybe, we were onto something after all. One could always hope!

Day 56: Born to be Wild!

Location: Applying for citizenship in Colombo, Sri Lanka

Having wasted so much time goofing off, we decided to get out of Colombo ASAP. Since we required a license to drive around Sri Lanka, we went to the Department of Motor Traffic – Werahera branch in Boralasgamuwa and in a couple of hours, we had the documents. We headed to Negambo to meet Mr. Suranga Perera, the owner of Sha Lanka for the motorcycles. Since our planned route involved a lot of off-roading, we decided to take a closer look at the *Baja*.

The man definitely knew his stuff. He looked at our plan and gave us detailed information on road conditions, weather, places to see, and as a bonus gave us a detailed road map of Sri Lanka. The Honda XR 250R *Baja* was a four-stroke, 249 cc enduro motorcycle capable of putting out 20 hp at 8100 rpm through a six-speed transmission. I took one of the *Bajas* out for a trial run and knew that this was the motorcycle, which I wanted to drive across the country. We worked out a deal and picked up the gear – helmets, safety gear and bungee cords to secure our bags.

Since all of us were desperate to hit the highway, we headed out immediately towards Chilaw, even though it was quite late in the day. The *Baja* was a dream to drive (yes, drive). Considering that she weighed a mere 125 kg, it took me a while to get used to her power and responsiveness, but after that it was a blast driving, especially when opening the throttle up in sixth gear. She cruised along beautifully and responded perfectly to every burst of power demanded of her. I was in love! Being used to Indian driving conditions, driving here felt natural to us. We just stuck to the golden rules:

1) Anything bigger than you, wants to and will run you over, given a chance.
2) Driving and overtaking on the wrong side is the right thing to do.

3) If by any odd chance you have functional headlights, use them only to blind oncoming traffic.
4) When receiving directions, '*seedha*' or '*thoda door*' means the guy doesn't have a clue.
5) Expect the unexpected – double overtakes, animals, uber aggressive driving, manic Tuk Tuks, a circus bear on a motorcycle.
6) Give the finger to pedestrians trying to cross the road, by either pretending you are invisible or by trying to stop your motorcycle through '*hand brakes*'. If they seriously believed that they could stop a motorcycle by raising their hand, there wouldn't be any need for brakes. Would there?
7) Animals are secretly masochistic; if you see them patiently sitting at the edge of the road, expect them to run across at the last possible moment and stick a foot or a tail under the motorcycle's wheel.
8) When two bus drivers decide to play *race-race*, get the hell off the road, far off the road.

We reached Chilaw by 6 p.m., and headed straight to the Munneswaram temple, the first of the sites related to the Ramayana that we planned to visit. Located two kilometres from Chilaw, it was the place where Lord Rama sensed that the effects of *Brahmana Dosham* were weak, and prayed to Lord Shiva for a solution.

The temple complex consisted of several smaller temples, with the chief one dedicated to Lord Shiva. We noticed that that the temple had a festive atmosphere to it; it was decorated with flowers and completely lit up with lamps and lights. Though it was filled with devotees, there was no pushing or shoving and despite our shabby appearance, people welcomed us with smiles. We offered our prayers and noticed an odd custom in this temple; the offerings to the Gods were watermelons, papayas, oranges, bananas, apples, and a dozen other types of fruits. Apparently, this was the norm in temples across Sri Lanka.

After our prayers, we drove into Chilaw and crashed at the Chilaw City Hotel in a nice air-conditioned room with access to the swimming pool and complementary breakfast. The room cost us 2000 SLR, quite cheap because it was off-season and because we used a few bargaining tricks that we had picked up from Xin and Chun.

Day one of our test had passed without any real result. While Sri could argue that we got the *Baja* because we trusted Suranga, practically speaking, it was just a standard deal. We would have got the *Baja* either way. Sam decided to keep an actual scorecard to see how this would turn out. He could be crudely analytical at times. Sigh.

Humanity 0 – 0 Misanthropy.

Day 57: I'm perfectly sane. But then, 94% of psychotics think they're perfectly sane. So I guess we have to ask ourselves, 'what is sane?' That's a good question.

Location: Chilaw, Sri Lanka

The next morning, we went to visit the Manavari Sivan Kovil (Eswaran Kovil), located ten kilometres north of Chilaw. This was the first Shiva Linga that Lord Rama installed to get rid of the *Brahmana Dosham*. The priest greeted us warmly, invited us in, and told us the importance of the temple – the Shiva Linga present in the temple was established by Lord Rama himself and hence is known as the *Ramalingam*. Since it is believed that Lord Rama was born in 5114 BCE, the Shiva Linga would be more than seven thousand years old. The priest performed a puja and pointed out various places in Sri Lanka, related to Lord Hanuman and the Ramayana.

After the puja, we resumed our journey towards Mannar and reached the Wilpattu national park after a few hours of peaceful cruising on the motorcycle. Wilpattu is one of the largest national parks in Sri Lanka covering over 130,000 hectares. The park has numerous *Villus* (lakes) from which it gets its name. It is also famous for its leopard and elephant populations, both of which gather around these lakes at dusk and dawn.

At the entrance, there was a border security post manned by the Sri Lankan Navy. They had a couple of bases and several high security areas in Wilpattu and checked all vehicles passing through the park. As soon as they saw my passport, they let us through with a friendly wave. That was always the case since we arrived in Sri Lanka. The people were friendly and warm and after they found out that we were Indians, they became even more welcoming.

A single dirt road ran through the heart of Wilpattu, along which all major traffic from Mannar to Colombo passed. Several smaller paths branched off the grand dirt road and led to various ponds, watchtowers, military camps, and historical places. Technically, all traffic was restricted to the main road, but since checks were non-existent, people could do whatever they pleased, as long as they were ok with the risks – land mines, wild animals, and being shot on sight.

The *Baja* had been running smoothly and the more I drove, the more I understood her subtleties. She was capable of insane bursts of power when demanded, good braking, and had brilliant manoeuvrability, but only if the centre of gravity was close to the engine. To address this, I decided to carry my bag on my back as opposed to securing it to the back of the motorcycle, as it offered a better centre of gravity, and in turn better manoeuvrability on these dirt roads. Sri and Sam preferred to have the bags attached with bungee cords. Amateurs.

There is no feeling in the world that compares to opening up the throttle of a motorcycle on a dirt road – the wind in your hair, adrenaline pumping, and your balls in your throat. Well, at least that's how I felt, as I sped down the main road, weaving around the occasional stone, bush, or pothole, and braking desperately when required. I even had a couple of spectacular crashes, especially one in which I ended halfway up a thorny scrub. In short, it was awesome! The only downside being the painful set of choices I faced afterwards – so I stick my hand on this thorn to get my foot out and I put my foot on this thorn to get my elbow free and so on so forth, ad infinitum.

Much to the annoyance of my companions, I declared that no side road would be considered off limits, especially those that led to ponds or ancient ruins. We spent plenty of time exploring these roads and I had a lot of fun, leaning into corners, speeding up, and quickly changing direction or shifting weight to avoid obstacles. Not knowing what was past the next corner, only added to the excitement. The best dirt road was the one that led to the ruins of the Pallekandal church, which had plenty of tight curves, low hanging branches, ramps, sand traps, and gravel. Sam didn't like it one bit, he said it disturbed the animals, but considering how close we were to the main road it wouldn't have made much of a difference.

We felt excited as we explored places off the beaten path. How long had it been since people were last here? What would we find? We felt like modern day Indiana Jones' on the quest for the new and improved Holy Grail. It was exciting and fun, as the old man had taught us – some of the best times are all in our heads.

Eventually, we got out of Wilpattu and headed towards Talaimannar, the geographically closest point to India and the other end of *Rama Setu*. This was when we saw our first serious face in Sri Lanka, I guess the closer you get to a war zone the more serious people get. Waves were returned with serious faces and the Special Task Force (STF) stopped us on more than one occasion. Once we explained what we were doing, they were quite cool about it and let us through.

So there we were cruising along past check points until we finally saw the Talaimannar lighthouse. It looked as if it was located behind a military base so we followed the road straight into the base. No sooner had we reached the gate than half a dozen soldiers popped out and surrounded us. The fact that they had automatic weapons trained on us didn't help us one bit in our explanation. They asked us many questions, checked our passports, and finally told us that we had to go around the base to get to the lighthouse. We were lucky that they we hadn't been shot. If we had done this a few years back, during the civil war, in all likelihood we would have!

While we hadn't been shot, we still had people with guns trained on us, ready to kill. Not particularly confidence inspiring. This didn't in any way look good for Sri. Yes, people were nice to us, they smiled and waved at us, but there wasn't anything that went above and beyond the call of niceness. Heck, we had a lot more inspiring incidents during our trek in India but since we decided not to count them, it was still **Humanity 0 – 0 Misanthropy.**

After a long day, we headed back to town and learnt that Mannar had a shortage of places to stay. We eventually found a room at 'The Lucky Rest Inn' for 400 SLR.

Day 58: You've got to ask yourself one question: 'Do I feel lucky?' Well, do ya, punk?

Location: Mannar, Sri Lanka

By 7 a.m., we were standing in front of a Baobab tree in Pallimundai. This was no ordinary Baobab; at 19.51 metres, the tree had the largest circumference in Sri Lanka. Yes, we had finally arrived in life. I turned around to find a couple of donkeys staring at me, no not Sam and Sri. Actual donkeys! Apparently, some merchants from Arabia thought that it would be a good idea to introduce donkeys and Baobabs in Sri Lanka. Inspired ideas like this were what brought the Brown Tree Snake to Guam and the Cane Toad to Australia and destroyed local ecosystems. We wondered what else we would run into, Kangaroos and Crocodile Dundee maybe.

Our next stop was the Thiruketheeswaram temple – the second of the three *Ramayana* Shiva Lingas in Sri Lanka, where Lord Rama offered prayers as penance for the *Brahmana Dosham*. Legend has it that this temple was built by Ravana's father-in-law, Mayan, the master architect, who also built the *Mayasabha* at Indraprastha.

The Portuguese destroyed this temple and it was only restored in the early 1900's, after the original Shiva Linga was excavated. Before it was destroyed, it was supposed to be the largest of the Shiva temples in Lanka. Considering that the Mannar Fort, the churches in Mannar, and the Hammershield Fort at Kayts were built with stones from the demolished temple, we could imagine how huge the original temple was.

Once at the temple, we saw multiple courtyards with various idols dedicated to the gods. The entrances to these courtyards were all lined up facing east and as we stood at the entrance of the temple, we saw the Shiva Linga past the doorways.

The doorways were decorated with lamps and it made for an astonishingly beautiful sight. We entered the temple, offered our prayers, and sat down to take in the peacefulness of the place.

After the puja, we planned to take a rather long detour through Madhu Road Sanctuary, Silavatturai, and Wilpattu to get to Anuradhapura. The road through Madhu Road Sanctuary was almost exclusively a dirt track as expected and we had plenty of fun, until we came across a '*Danger – Mines*' sign smack in the middle of the road. The sign had pictures of several types of mines and instructions on whom to contact in case we ran into one. Yeah, we would collect the mine plus whatever was left of our body parts and definitely call the number. Since there was no other traffic on the road, we weren't sure if it was actually safe to proceed or not. Eventually, I drove forward, shitting bricks at each loud noise that the motorcycle made as it passed over gravel and twigs. Although he wouldn't admit it, it showed in Sam's demeanour; he was scared shitless as well.

Fortunately, we didn't get blown to bits and drove into Anuradhapura at 2 p.m. It was one of the ancient capitals of Lanka and is a UNESCO World Heritage Site. It is part of Sri Lanka's *cultural triangle,* which consists of Anuradhapura, Polonnaruwa, Ritigala, Medirigiriya, Kandy, Sigiriya, and Dambulla. These sites are famous for their collections of ancient ruins, *dagobas* (huge semi-circular structure containing religious relics), temples, and other monuments.

There was plenty to see here including the Sri Maha Bodhi (Sacred Bo Tree), the Ruwanweliseya Dagoba, Atamasthana (Eight Great Places of Veneration), and the remnants of the ancient city of Anuradhapura. The Ruwanweliseya Dagoba, at 338 feet was one of the tallest monuments in the world. It was so huge that we could see it from a distance of over ten kilometres and as we got closer, we watched it get bigger and bigger, until we were at its base. It was our first time seeing a large Dagoba (no

Googling remember) and we stood there silently in awe. How strong would their faith have been, to dream of and construct a monument of such size and splendour, we wondered.

We headed towards the Sri Maha Bodhi, which is one of the oldest documented trees in the world. More importantly, it is a part of the Bodhi tree, under which Prince Siddhartha meditated and attained enlightenment, becoming '*The Buddha*'. Sanghamitra, the daughter of King Ashoka brought a branch of the tree from Bodh Gaya to Sri Lanka. We had expected to see a huge tree in a large garden, what we instead saw were a few branches of the tree peeking over a couple of huge walls. We could not tell how big it was as it was almost completely hidden behind the wall. The wall and the security for the tree was put in place, after a madman tried to cut it down and the LTTE carried out an attack on it.

There were several monks and people sitting around the tree praying or meditating and we joined them. We ran into a monk here, with whom we started talking to about Buddhist and Hindu paths to salvation.

Eventually, I asked a question that was on my mind, "Why do good people seem to suffer more than evil people?"

"Suffering is relative. For a baby, a pinch may cause excruciating pain, whereas for an adult it is brushed aside. For some people a harsh word causes more suffering than a physical blow. How does one measure suffering?"

"Why do good people need to suffer in the first place?" Sri asked.

"Light is appreciated only after one sees darkness. Without it, one can never truly understand the value of light. The suffering that people undergo only serves to sweeten the happiness that follows. Only one that has truly suffered can truly enjoy happiness."

"That can't always be the case. What about the case of a child, who has cancer and dies. He doesn't experience happiness," Sam protested.

"That is because you see life as a singular event and not as a cycle of birth and death."

"Yeah, take the easy way out. Cycles are convenient to ride. Aren't they?" Sam muttered under his breath.

"So this child will receive happiness in his next birth?"

"That would be based on his karma."

"Why do we have to suffer so many times? I mean, if we see the darkness once, isn't it etched in our memory forever?" was Sri's next question.

"The human mind is fickle and has a tendency to forget harsh times and as a result we always tend to forget our suffering. It is a coping mechanism to look forward in life, but it also works against us."

"I see. So there is no escaping from suffering?"

"Meditation offers the path to break out of this cycle."

We had reached the stage, where old men, priests, and sages walking in randomly, sharing their wisdom, and continuing on their way was a normal occurrence. We didn't even bat an eyelid and carried on as if nothing happened. After a quick visit to the Lowamahapaya (Brazen Palace), we headed into town for dinner.

We entered a small restaurant where we ran into a woman, who insisted that she knew someone who looked just like me. Since she was the owner of the place, we got special treatment and plenty of food – fish, chicken, fried rice, *Kottu* (shredded parota salad of sorts), Milo, and yoghurt.

Sri decided that this was a +1 for humanity and the discussion with the monk was another +1. Sam said that neither would count since one was a conversation and the other was due to a coincidence. I watched in disbelief as they haggled over their belief in humanity over +1s before they finally dragged me in and insisted that I make the decision. This is how I scored it –

Humanity 1 – 0 Misanthropy.

Although the monk might have taught us out of kindness, it was his duty to preach the *Dhamma;* so technically, it was a neutral action. The woman in the restaurant could have just given us the food we ordered and gone about her business. Instead, she went out of her way to cook us a hearty meal and made sure we were happy. Definitely an act of kindness in my books.

Day 59: In brightest day, in blackest night, No evil shall escape my sight.

Location: Anuradhapura, Sri Lanka

The food in Sri Lanka seemed familiar because of the ingredients used, but was quite different from Indian food at the same time. It had a similar taste, thanks to the spices and masala, but the same dishes were prepared in completely different ways. Apart from the usual suspects like rice, dal, roti, and curry, we had eaten *String hoppers* (weird looking parathas made of thin wiry noodles), *Kottu*, spicy mutton, *Sambola* (coconut-based chutney of sorts), jackfruit curry, squid, and a hundred types of fishes (yes, they eat plenty of fish). We also had brilliant desserts like sweet yoghurt, *Balatur* (three-layered sweet with ice cream, fruit, Sherbet, and dragon fruit), Faluda, and an assortment of cakes and biscuits.

Everything looked enticing and there were so many varieties of food available that deciding what to eat always took us forever, *"I want what the person next to me is having. On second thoughts, the person behind me is having something interesting too; think I will have that instead. Oh and perhaps that fish curry and Kottu as well. Dammit, just get me one of everything you have on the menu!"* Considering the quantities we were devouring, we would probably have to be rolled out of Sri Lanka by the time the trip would be done.

After yet another heavy breakfast, we headed to the Anuradhapura Museum to get the Cultural Triangle passes, where we ran into a guide. As per our commitment, we decided to trust the guide, who promptly advised us to skip the museum. This was possibly the worst advice we received and followed during the entire trip. He then led us on a blitzkrieg tour of Anuradhapura and in a span of three hours, managed to rush us through a bunch of places like the Mirisawetiya Dagoba, Ruwanweliseya, Thuparama Dagoba, Jetewanarama,

Twin ponds, Samadhi Statue, Elephant Pond, *Moonstone*, Ratna Prasada (chapter house), and the Abhayagiri Dagoba.

Initially, all he did was read out what was written on the various plaques and glare at us, if we looked around for too long. He wasn't too enthusiastic and didn't seem to know much either, but when Sam subtly hinted that he was looking to pick up a gem for his girlfriend, the guide got excited and stepped up his game. At every site that we visited after that, the guide gave out detailed information and ran around us like a lost puppy. People could be so naïve and greedy. This guy definitely didn't help inspire any confidence in people. We eventually grew tired of his antics, promised him that we would buy the gem from his cousin in Kandy, and shooed him off. We leisurely explored a few other places like the Lankarama Dagoba, Burma temple, and Nuwara Wewa before deciding to head back.

Each of us had our personal favourites from the tour; Sri loved the *Moonstone*, a semi-circular stone slab with intricate carvings of flames, creepers, animals, swans, and lotuses in concentric semicircles representing spiritual progress from *samsara* to *nirvana*. Sam liked the Abhayagiri Dagoba, as it showed what the dagobas looked like originally, without any whitewash. My personal favourite was the sight of the Jetwanarama at night. With the lights on, it looked breath taking and offered a deeper, mystical view.

After the visit, the *Baja* took the opportunity to give me a hard time. She didn't start up and no matter how many times I tried she refused to comply. I even tried pushing her to jump start her, but it didn't work. Sri and Sam watched me with growing impatience for fifteen minutes after which they snapped.

"You left the light on when we went inside. Didn't you?" Sam asked accusingly.

"Maybe we should have rented him a bicycle. Oh wait, that's probably too much for him, a tricycle would be more appropriate," Sri said.

"Yeah that would have been payback for the bicycle tools that he brought on the Manali **motorcycle** trip."

"It's easy to blame me for everything. You guys have messed up equally if not more."

"Oh, really?"

"Do you remember the time we took that drive down the west coast and the car broke down? Let me remind you of what you did. You opened up the engine, identified the problem, and poured water into the *radiator,* until all the black goo came out. Except it wasn't the radiator, was it? It was the friggin *oil tank* that you guys poured water down. Geniuses. And you are ones to talk."

Thanks to the guide, it was now **Humanity 1 – 1 Misanthropy.**

Day 60: Run, my pretty little chunks of XP! Run!

Location: Anuradhapura, Sri Lanka

The next morning, we started driving towards Trincomalee (Trinco), which was one of the major ports of Sri Lanka. The name Trincomalee was derived from the Thirukonamalai Konesar Kovil, the most famous of the Shiva temples in Sri Lanka and the last one on our checklist. Along the way, we also planned to visit Mihintale, a pilgrimage site considered as the birthplace of Buddhism in Sri Lanka. King Ashoka sent his son Mahinda to spread the faith and it was at Mihintale that Arahat Mahinda met King Devanampiyatissa and preached the Dhamma, thus establishing Buddhism in Lanka.

Mihintale is located on top of a hill known as *Missaka Pabbata* and despite the challenge in getting up there (pilgrims had to climb a total of 1840 steps to get to the top), there were plenty of people both young and old, who were making the ascent. The Ambasthala Dagoba was built by King Makalantissa to mark the spot where Mahinda met King Devanampiyatissa. The views from the Maha Stupa were amazing and we could see all the way to Anuradhapura.

We continued our journey and after a few hours of driving in the hot sun reached Nilavali, which was twenty kilometres from Trinco. All the diving camps were located in Nilavali and we talked to a few diving groups to set up a dive to Pigeon Island for us. We finally chose to go with 'Trinco Water Sports', and haggled down the price to 8000 SLR per person, for a single dive, snorkelling, park permit fees and the boat ride to Pigeon Island.

We settled in the 'Aqua Inns Hotel' located right next door and had a talk with the dive master about the plan. After we were done, he introduced us to a friend of his to show us around the place. As we started talking, we found out that the guy was a part time *beach boy*. There are many young men in Sri Lanka who, for lack of better opportunities depended on the tourism industry for survival. Quite a few of them had taken to prostitution and they hung out around the beach resorts hoping to get picked up by foreign women. If they got lucky, they would earn enough money to see themselves and their families through the season, if not, tomorrow was another day.

We headed out to a beach shack and he told us his story. He had no job and his only source of income was guiding and beach boy-ing. He said that he didn't like it, but had no other choice. That was when he got a call from his American girlfriend, who he proceeded to talk to for the next half an hour. Later, he told us that he had three foreign girlfriends, who would fly down for their vacations and spend time and money on him. He said that he would be fine when they were around, but once they left, he would be left with nothing but his troubles.

All of a sudden, the boy decided that it was time to get to work. He spotted a couple of women sitting at a table across the bar and proceeded to ask them in a loud voice, "Hey do you need some company?"

The women looked at each other but didn't reply and the boy decided that he needed to provide additional incentive.

"This guy," he said pointing at me, "is from India and he knows the Kama Sutra in and out."

The women laughed and politely declined. We were left flabbergasted, until Sam burst out laughing and said, "Look at the beach boy pimp our hero out. Looks like everybody can read it on your face."

We debated if the incident counted as a +1 for misanthropy, but in the end decided not to consider it, since we weren't affected by it in any way. The score remained at **Humanity 1 – 1 Misanthropy** and I wondered if this was really going anywhere.

Day 61: Die Me, Dichotomy

Location: Trincomalee, Sri Lanka

Diving Day! All through the pre dive instruction, I was nervous. While I loved the water, I still had the grand inheritance from my childhood – my fear of sharks keeping me company. After the instruction, a boat picked us and took us to Pigeon Island, called so because of the thousands of Rock Pigeons that called the island home.

We carried the tanks, put on our wetsuits, masks, and weights and headed into the water, where we had a quick refresher course. As soon as we dived, we noticed that a majority of the corals at Pigeon Island were bleached, an indicator of poor reef health. It was infuriating to swim in a reef devoid of the colour and diversity we had seen at other dive sites like the Andamans. We saw a variety of marine life like eels, starfish, lobsters, sea cucumbers, and clams, but it was still disappointing. After an hour, we were done with the dive and headed back in frustration. The dive instructor must have noticed our frustration (not that we particularly tried to hide it) and recommended a spot for us to snorkel.

We jumped in and two minutes later, found ourselves almost face to face with a Blacktip reef shark. It was around 6 feet long and despite my fear of sharks, I didn't feel threatened in any way, possibly because I knew it couldn't kill me in one bite. Maybe if it had been bigger, I would have thought otherwise. We watched for a few minutes, as it swam in circles looking for prey and abruptly left. Immediately afterwards, we spotted a Green Sea turtle and swam along with it for a while. Eventually, it tired of us and with a *whoosh* of its flippers swam away leaving us desperately trying to catch up. Swimming with sharks and turtles made up for the lacklustre scuba experience and it was an incredible feeling swimming with those magnificent creatures.

A while later, we were back at the hotel and in the afternoon, we decided to visit Tiriyaya. It was an ancient Buddhist site and seaport, located approximately forty kilometres north of Trinco, and is one of the holiest places in Sri Lanka. Legend states that after the Buddha achieved enlightenment, two merchants – Tapussa and Bhallika, offered him alms for the first time. He taught them the Dhamma and gave them a few strands of his hair, which they carried along with them all the way to Sri Lanka. On a visit to Girikanda (now Tiriyaya), they realised that this was a holy place and established a shrine with the Buddha's hair. At a later point of time, the *Akasacetiya* (Sky Stupa or Stupa in the Sky) and the *Vatadage* (circular building to protect the shrine) were established.

After an hour of driving, we were at Tiriyaya and it was a short trek up the hill to where the Stupa was. We were followed up the hill by a dog, which after a while we ended up following.

It reminded us of a dog, which guided us up a hill on the Kechopari Lake trek in Sikkim. Once we reached the top of the hill, the dog jumped through the shrubbery and kept barking at us to follow. Since it was nearly dark, we didn't want to risk taking a new path down especially an unused one, so we headed back on the path we came up the mountain. All the way down, we kept shouting to guide the dog towards us and the dog kept barking to guide us down. After a while, the dog stopped barking and we were worried that a leopard or a bear had eaten it up.

We sat down, quite depressed at the thought of losing a companion and friend. That's how we regarded her, even though our acquaintance was short and wondered how we were going to explain to its owners that we had managed to **lose** a guide dog. We started speaking epitaphs of the great one, when all of a sudden, we turned around to find a pissed off dog trying to bite our legs off for leaving it behind.

Since we did not want a repeat of that, we kept a close eye on this dog and followed it wherever it led us. Hey come on! He acted as if he wanted to show us something and he did – an ancient stone tablet with an inscription. After revealing this secret to us, he nonchalantly led us up the hill.

The top of the hill was flat and had the Akasacetiya, Vatadage, Shrines, Moonstones, and *Guardstones*. The Stupa and Vatadage predate Anuradhapura and are considered architectural marvels, as they are near perfection with no jutting edges or gaps. We sat there and watched the sunset over Anuradhapura. It is said that as we die the most beautiful moments of our life flash before our eyes. This moment would certainly be in that slide show.

Humanity 1 – 1 Misanthropy and introducing a new competitor – Dogeism with +1 for a three way tie.

Day 62: The Ramans do everything in threes

Location: Trincomalee, Sri Lanka

Thirukonamalai Konesar Kovil aka the Koneswaram Kovil is a *Maha Shakti Peetha* and the last of the Ramayana related Shiva Lingas that we planned to visit in Sri Lanka. This temple is also referred to as *Dakshina Kailasam* (Kailash of the south), as it is located on the exact longitude as Mount Kailash (home of Lord Shiva). The temple is located on a hill, which overlooks the harbour, the town, and all surrounding areas and the views it offers are simply brilliant.

An ancient temple, it finds mention in both the Ramayana and the Mahabharata. Under the patronage of a series of Chola kings, it grew rapidly and had a huge Gopuram with a thousand pillars. With every rise comes a fall and in 1622 the temple was destroyed by the Portuguese. It was only reconstructed after the idols of Lord Shiva, Parvathi and Ganesh were found buried underground. Later in 1956, the famed author, Arthur C. Clarke and photographer, Mike Wilson discovered the legendary *Swayambhu lingam,* while scuba diving and it was enshrined.

After our temple visit and *puja,* we proceeded towards Minneriya town for lunch. We decided to take a drive around Minneriya Wewa to see elephants and if we got lucky, witness 'The Gathering' (during the dry season hundreds of elephants from across Sri Lanka *gather* at Minneriya to feast on the grass, mate, play, and interact with each other). Near the lake, we spotted a lone elephant, so we parked off the road and sat under a tree, watching it eat and drink.

This was when we ran into a herdsman, tending his cattle. Being a local, he knew the ways of the forest and animals and was kind enough to take us closer to the elephant. We stopped at a distance of eight hundred metres, while he walked around the lake, gathering his cows. He was least bothered by the elephant, which kept making false charges at him from barely fifty metres away.

The elephant wasn't what we should have been worried about. The herdsman had a bull – a huge bugger that stood around 6 feet tall, which suddenly decided that it did not like our presence there and charged at us! Since it was an open field, we had nowhere to run and considering its size, one hit would have definitely broken a few bones. We did the only thing that was logically possible; we ran and positioned ourselves (read hid) behind the herdsman. The bull was apprehensive about charging at its master and tried to circle around him and attack us. We followed suit and ensured that the herdsman was always between the bull and us. After a few minutes of playing *Hide-and-seek,* the herdsman decided enough was enough, caught the bull, and tied it up. We taunted it after it was tied up and returned to our tree, awaiting the arrival of the elephant herd.

I started reading a book, while occasionally glancing at the solitary elephant, when I heard the desperate squealing of tires from the road behind us.

"Moronic drivers. Who the hell is braking so hard on these empty highways?" I wondered aloud.

"Phiaow."

"Did you hear that?" Sam asked.

"What?" Sri asked.

Stop making funny noises Sri," Sam said.

"It wasn't me," was his response.

"PHIAOWWWWW!"

All of us turned in unison in the direction of the noise, "An elephant!" I exclaimed in panic.

"Run!" Sam exclaimed.

"NO! Do not run. It's barely thirty feet away; it will easily catch and pummel us," Sri said.

"Let me quickly take a picture. We are never going to get this close to an elephant in the wild again," I said.

"Are you insane? If the flash goes off, it's going to kill us!"

"It hasn't displayed any signs of aggression, no false charge, or trumpeting," Sri replied.

"I can get a quick snap."

"Phiaow?" was what the elephant thought about that idea and it made sure we knew of it, with a raised trunk.

"That does it. We are out of here! Just walk slowly into that huge bush to our left," Sri said.

Luckily, for us the bush was close enough for us to shuffle awkwardly behind. Unfortunately, the elephant panicked and decided to run around the bush as well. If we continued on the same path, we would soon be face-to-face with a panicked elephant. Definitely not what we wanted, so we quickly dove into the bush and luckily for us, she ran past and we managed to survive. Our hearts were racing and it was a while, before we calmed down and figured out our next course of action. Staying there was stupid and unsafe.

This was when Sri came up with a brilliant idea that we climb a tree and watch the elephants as they passed underneath us. It was a 'dumb as a brick' idea, but since nobody objected, we climbed a twenty-five foot tree. In the process, I managed to crush a pack of yoghurt that I had in my pack and it spilled all over the camera, GPS and maps. Since we weren't carrying any water, I was forced to spend the next thirty minutes licking everything clean.

"Wherever there is stupidity, you will find us. Wherever there is pig-headedness, we'll be there. Wherever kittens are threatened, you will find...The Three Amigos!" Sam exclaimed.

At dusk, a herd of elephants did arrive and walked past the tree. It was exhilarating to see the huge beasts from such a close distance and was definitely worth all the trouble. Eventually, we climbed down and headed into Minneriya town.

Thanks to the herdsman, who was kind enough to take us to the elephant and protect us from a charging bull, it was now - **Humanity 2 - 1 Misanthropy.**

Day 63: Stay a while and listen!

Location: Minneriya, Sri Lanka

Polonnaruwa was the second ancient capital of Sri Lanka and a World Heritage site. If you had time to visit only one place in the Cultural Triangle, then this should be it. There is so much to see – huge statues, palaces, frescos, *Viharas* (monastery), Guardstones, Moonstones, Vatadages, baths, tanks, cave art, and several other relics.

We went to the Polonnaruwa archaeological centre to pick up some guide maps and ran into Mr. Gunawardhana, a guide with over a decade of experience. After our bad experience with the guide in Anuradhapura, we were sceptical, but since we had our *'humanity vs misanthropy'* experiment, we decided to take a chance. Our gamble paid off and we quickly found out that the man was a walking-talking encyclopaedia of Sri Lanka's heritage sites.

He started the tour with a detailed explanation of the various artefacts in the archaeological museum. This was the first time that we did not get bored in a museum. It had the usual collection of statues, drawings, maps, coins, household artefacts, weapons and other stuff, but what actually drew us in were the models of the various sites showing what they must have looked like in their prime. This was what we had missed in Anuradhapura! Dammit.

After the museum, we visited various heritage structures like the King's palace, the *Dalada Maluwa*, Thuparama (an image house) and the Sathmahal Prasada (seven-storied mini pyramid of sorts with elements of Cambodian architecture). Even though Sam generally hated seeing religious or historical buildings, he still loved the place, probably because there was so much new to see here. The first time a person sees something new, they experience a rush of childlike curiosity and wonder.

We spent a lot of time at each of the sites and at 6 p.m., went around looking for a place to stay. We found the *Manel* guesthouse, settled in, and headed to the in-house restaurant. We ordered some food and I was about to start writing, when I heard a loud conversation followed by rambunctious laughter. It came from two women, who had occupied the table right behind us. Why couldn't they have picked any of the other tables? Sigh. Thanks to the racket, we couldn't write or read a single word. After a few minutes, Sam decided to take things into his own hands and asked them to tone it down a little. They refused and made a counter offer – they asked us to join them. Since we had nothing better to do, we politely accepted their invitation.

They were from Russia and they had an interesting story. The previous day, they had been sitting in a bar in Moscow drinking and were bored to death. That was when they decided to do a trip; they pulled out a world map, randomly put a finger on Sri Lanka, headed straight to the airport, and ended up here. All their clothes were purchased once they reached Colombo. It was surprising how spontaneous people could be!

Over a long conversation, they gave us an entirely different perspective of travelling and living – of going to places randomly, having random conversations with strangers, and of doing things as they came up. Travelling with no expectations or plans often produced the sweetest of results they said. It was completely different from our approach to a trip (we had taken over a year to plan our trip) and that gave us something to think about. I doubted whether I could ever manage a trip like that considering my obsession with checking things off lists. I would probably go mad without a checklist.

The best places to visit are ones no one cares about, and the best plans are the ones never made.

As it turned out, they weren't innocent or naïve either. They had sweet-talked the beach boys at the hotel into getting them maps, *arrack,* and bicycles. All through our conversation, the boys kept trying to jump in and hit on the women but were ignored. Once that didn't work, they got pissed at us instead of at the women. Perfectly logical, the best solution when you mess up is to blame someone else for your mistakes.

+1 to Humanity for the guide who went out of his way to make our experience memorable, +1 for the women to invite us for dinner and for their willingness to share their story, and +1 to Misanthropy for the beach boys, who got angry at us for no fault of ours. **Humanity 3 - 2 Misanthropy.**

Days 64 to 66: You couldn't lead ant-droids to a picnic

Location: Sigiriya, Dambulla, and Kandy, Sri Lanka

Over the next couple of days, we visited other areas of the Cultural Triangle like Sigiriya, Pidurangala, Dambulla, and Kandy.

Sigiriya (Lion's Rock) is a World Heritage site and ancient capital of Sri Lanka. It certainly is unique, thanks to its location – it is built on a huge rock, 180 metres high. There were several things to see like the Royal Gardens, the Mirror wall, Lion staircase, and the Sigiriya Frescos – paintings of *Apsaras* (celestial nymphs).

The Golden Temple of Dambulla aka Dambulla Rock temple is one of the oldest Buddhist temples in Sri Lanka and yet another World Heritage site. King Abhaya built it in the 1st century BCE and it has more than eighty caves, five of which are especially renowned for their paintings and 157 statues of the Buddha.

The 'Sri Dalada Maligawa' or the Temple of the Tooth as it is popularly known as, is to Buddhists what Varanasi, Mecca, or Jerusalem is to their respective religions. It holds a tooth (canine) of the Buddha and is the most visited place in Sri Lanka.

While all of these places were amazing, the place that we found most interesting was one we stumbled upon by chance – the Aluthnuwara Dewalaya, located just off the Kandy highway. At first glance, it seemed like a typical temple but it is not – it is a place of worship for both Hindus and Buddhists. The Stupa and the Temple are within the same compound, almost next to each other and many people went around offering prayers at both places. You see sights like this and wonder why religion isn't used as a unifying force and is instead used to separate people. You would think with places like this, there wouldn't have been a damn war.

+1 to Humanity for the people praying in peace together despite the civil war and all the evil and negativity it brought with it. **Humanity 4 - 2 Misanthropy.**

Day 67: If the thought of it seems crazy – you weren't crazy enough to begin with.

Location: Kandy, Sri Lanka

The elephant orphanage at Pinnawala is located about thirty kilometres from Kandy on the road to Colombo. At the orphanage, there were around ninety elephants including calves, a lot of which had sad stories. Most of the elephants were orphans, abandoned by their mothers and raised here; a few others were born here. One of the saddest stories was that of Sama, an elephant who had lost her leg due to the war. The sight of her struggling along on three legs could bring the coldest hearts to tears, but then again, who was responsible for her misery, but the most savage of all animals.

The elephants here *seemed* to be well cared for and the entire show revolved around this – feeding the adult elephants grass, feeding milk to the baby elephants, and giving them baths in the river across the street. The circus started at 8:30 a.m., with the baby elephants being fed milk from bottles by the visitors. After this, the elephants were taken down to the river for a wash and some fun. While they were herded to the river, visitors could buy elephant based products, take a free tour of the elephant dung paper-processing factory, or have a drink in any of the restaurants next to the river.

While we waited for the herd to arrive, Sam spoke up, "This place is depressing. Let's just get out of here."

"Yeah, Sama's condition was quite depressing," Sri replied.

"No. That's not it. It's the fact that the elephants are kept in captivity with very little freedom."

"Most of those elephants were rescued and would probably have died if left in the wild."

"Death is natural. Captivity isn't. Animals should never be kept captive."

"Zoos keep animals captive. Are you saying that all zoos are bad? Zoos allow people, especially children to gain a deeper understanding and appreciation of animals. They run breeding programs for endangered species, preventing species extinction and provide animals with security, food, and shelter. It's more than they could ask for. Given a choice, I think they would love to stay in zoos."

"I guess all those animals that are constantly trying to escape from zoos must have some sort of attention seeking personality disorder. If I was an endangered species, I would rather live for a day in the wild, than a lifetime in a zoo for a breeding program."

"You have been brainwashed into believing that freedom is the most important thing in life; even above survival."

"How about a taste of your own medicine? Let me quote Sigmund Freud, *'Most people do not really want freedom, because freedom involves responsibility, and most people are frightened of responsibility'*."

Sri knew when he was beaten and backed down. Sam continued his tirade, "If only the animals resisted a little, they would have been far better off. Imagine if the Orcas at Sea World ate three or four trainers. They would pretty much assure the freedom of all other killer whales in the world."

"Where is the damned *Beastmaster,* when you need him?"

In the meantime, the elephants arrived at the river and we got back to watching the elephants. They were an unruly bunch, lifting hats from people passing by, stealing bananas, and pulling skirts. We watched as the elephants enjoyed their baths, but Sam's words remained in our heads and we left soon after. There was something about the place that made all of us uneasy – that things weren't as they appeared. We later found out that there were reports of the elephants being given away to private agencies. Sam was right, the minute you give up freedom for something else, you give up everything.

"God, grant me the serenity to accept the things I cannot change,
The courage to change the things I can,
And the wisdom to know the difference." - The Serenity Prayer

Our next objective was to trek up Sri Pada aka Adam's peak, for which we headed to the town of Nallitanniya, which served as the base camp for Adam's peak. The road from Aluthnuwara to Ramboda was atrocious; it wasn't a road with potholes, it was potholes with a little bit of road. It was a long two hours, before we made it through the bad stretch and my butt cheeks could finally relax.

We drove on, enjoying the sights and were close to Ramboda, when we saw a puppy sitting and wailing in the middle of the highway. We were already running late, but I still parked to the side, picked him up, and carried him to the side of the road. I bought him something to eat from a nearby shop and turned around, only to find the little bugger standing in the middle of the road again. Once again, I approached him, but this time he ran away. I tried to chase after him, but in my hurry, I was almost run over by a truck. In the few seconds it took for the truck to pass, the bugger disappeared. 'Had he been run over?' I wondered, until Sam pointed out that the puppy had run into a nearby house. I swear that if he had not run off, I would have killed him myself! This was when I noticed that a bunch of people standing on the other side of the road, laughing their asses off. I tried to salvage my pride (or whatever was left of it) by stepping into a restaurant for lunch. Dogs can be fun and endearing at times, but can also be a total pain in the ass at other times. We had lost thirty minutes in the wild puppy chase. Considering that it was 3:30 p.m., and it was a six-hour drive to Adam's peak, we were way behind schedule.

The Ramboda Sri Baktha Hanuman temple was perched high on the top of a hill and had a sixteen-foot idol of Lord Hanuman made out of granite. Under the gaze of the setting sun, the temple shone brightly, almost as if it was made entirely of gold and made for a magnificent sight. According to legend, this was the place where the two armies faced each other for the first time. Lord Rama's army on the Ramboda hillside and Ravana's on the other side, separated by the Ramboda Lake. Standing in front of the temple, we could imagine how the entire setting would have looked like with all the flags, banners, trumpets, and battle cries. We quickly offered our prayers and hit the road.

By 6 p.m., we were nowhere close to Nallitanniya and since it was in the hills, it got cold. My being dressed in flip-flops and shorts did not help my case and at one point, I had to count my fingers to ensure that they hadn't frozen and fallen off. We continued driving through the cold, reached Nuwara Eliya by 7:30 p.m., and two hours later, we were in Hutton. It was pitch dark, with no streetlights and absolutely nobody in sight to ask for directions. Luckily, we stumbled across a couple of signs that indicated the route to Adam's peak.

The only time we stopped was when I had an encounter with yet another dog. It was standing in the middle of the road and as I slowed down to avoid crashing into it, it turned around and chased me. I panicked, lost balance, and crashed on the side of the road. I was frustrated and tired from the exhausting ride and chased after the dog with a stick. Once I realised I couldn't catch it, I sat down and cursed the dog for a full five minutes until Sri and Sam helped me up and we continued onward.

Once again, the trip was wearing me down and bringing out my dark side. We all had our demons to deal with – Sam had *Moha* (delusion or temptation), Sri had *Lobh* (greed or attachment), and I took up the best ones – *Mada* (pride) and *Krodha* (anger or wrath). Sigh, even in my sins I took pride. Heck, if we took a closer look at ourselves, we could probably have added *Kama* (lust), *Matsarya* (envy or jealousy), hate, selfishness, gluttony, and sloth to ensure a full house in all religions. On the bright side, I guess at least we knew our sins and that was one-step towards stopping ourselves from succumbing to them.

"Anger is a killing thing: it kills the man who angers, for each rage leaves him less than he had been before – it takes something from him." - Louis L'Amour

We eventually reached Nallitanniya at around midnight and found that the entire town was asleep. Where would we stay we wondered? It was far too cold to stay outside. Just then, to our luck, we saw a light turn on at the River View Wathsala Inn. The manager had decided to take a leak at the exact moment that we passed by. We crashed at 12:30 p.m. and had to be up by 3 a.m., to start for Adam's Peak. Squirrel mode ON!

As we were about to fall asleep, Sri spoke up, "That was an extraordinary set of circumstances that brought us here. Our stopping twice because of dogs, making it the exact time that the manager was up."

"Don't you think that you are reading too much into this?" Sam asked.

"Maybe I am. Maybe I am not. Aren't you reading too little into this? Think about how many times we have had chance encounters on this trip. Even if you look at it statistically, the numbers are skewed in favour of what I am saying. Besides, you know what I am talking about. Embrace the dark side already brother. Fighting it only results in you getting worn out."

Dogeism was back with a bang. **Humanity 4, Misanthropy 2, and Dogeism 2.**

Day 68: I've got morons on my team

Location: Nallitanniya, Sri Lanka

Sri Pada aka Adam's Peak aka *Samanalakande* (Butterfly Mountain) is one of the highest peaks in Sri Lanka and at around 2,200 metres is significantly taller than Mahendragiri. It is said to have a sacred footprint of either Lord Shiva, the Buddha, or Adam (depending on who you are asking) etched on a rock at the summit and hence is considered to be a holy place. During peak season, thousands of pilgrims climb this mountain and the whole place becomes a *Kumbh Mela* of sorts. Luckily, for us, since it was off-season, we expected very few people on the mountain.

We were up by 3 a.m., and began our trek up the mountain. We were told that it takes around three hours to reach the top, so we were hoping to reach the summit by 5:45 a.m. and witness the sunrise. As soon as we reached the entrance to Sri Pada, there were two paths. As expected, we *chose poorly*, and by the time we backtracked and made it to the correct path it was 3:30 a.m. During the pilgrimage season, the marketplace would have been teeming with people, but at that point of time, it was just empty shops with wild boars and rats running around. We chose poorly at the next fork as well and ended up losing more time. Eventually at 3:45 a.m., we thought we had located the correct path. Five minutes later, we realised that we had gotten lost again. The situation was hopeless; the whole place was a maze and we were the mice!

Suddenly out of the dark, a hero rode in or rather trotted in on four legs. She was a brown and white stray and she seemed to point the way out for us. She would walk ahead a few steps, turn around and look at us, sort of indicating for us to follow. It was a little surprising, but who were we to look a gift dog in the mouth. We followed her and within thirty minutes, she had led us to the base of the mountain to a stairway that led all the way to the peak.

It was going to be simple now; all we had to do walk up the five thousand or so steps. Easy peasey. Since we were short on time, we pushed ourselves hard and soon found ourselves short of breath. The dog seemed to be having an especially hard time with our pace and was panting so hard that we worried that she would have a heart attack. Since we wouldn't have made it up without her help, we decided to take a break and get to the top together, even if it meant that we would miss the sunrise.

It was a hard climb and we had to stop to catch our breath every few minutes. Each step felt like a friggin wall and towards the end, as a grand finale there was a four hundred metre section, where each step was about a metre high. Mercifully, there were some railings in place to assist the pilgrims and we managed to crawl up to the peak by 5:40 a.m.

At the top, we found a layer of mist and clouds so thick that we couldn't even see our hands. We decided to wait for the sun to come up, hoping that it would clear up the clouds. We headed in to the complex to look at the footprint of God only to find the complex locked. We would find out later that it was only open during the peak season. Sam ranted for a long time while I petted and fed the dog.

We waited for a long time but it was to no avail. Even though the sun came up, the clouds were still too thick to see anything. In the right conditions, this was supposed to be one of the most beautiful sights that Sri Lanka had to offer. At sunrise, visitors could see a near perfect triangular shadow of the mountain, as the sun came up behind it. We would have been happy to see anything, but the climb was rewarding in itself and we had a blast doing it along with our new friend. **Humanity 4, Misanthropy 2, and Dogeism 3.**

A quick walk down the mountain and a wash later, we were on the road to Nuwara Eliya, where we crashed at the 'Lourdes Inn hotel' for some much needed R&R.

Day 69: I shall be waiting to reward your genius, or to have you beheaded for terminal stupidity!

Location: Nuwara Eliya, Sri Lanka

Our destination for the day was the Horton's Plains National Park, where we planned to see World's End (*Patal Lok* as per the Ramayana) and a few other sights. After a one and a half hour drive, we reached the entry point of the park. At the ticket counter, we walked in and noticed the insane premium for foreigners. In Sri Lanka, they follow a dual pricing policy at all major tourist spots and charge visitors through their noses and pretty much any other orifice they can. If locals were charged 50 SLR for an entry ticket, foreigners would have to pay around 2000 SLR for the same thing. The premium was truly insane and hence we decided that we would pretend to be Sri Lankan and sneak in.

As I stepped up, the ticket seller greeted me with the customary, "Ayubowan."

I greeted him back, "Ayubowan."

"Washa wusha entry?" was what I could make out of what he said next. I suppose that if I spoke in my mother tongue, it would sound the same way to him as well.

"Ow," I said with a nod, hoping that answered his question.

"You better end the conversation now. That's all of the Sinhalese you know!" Sri whispered.

"Wisha wausha camera pisha?" was his next question.

"Ow!" I replied and showed him the camera. This was quickly turning into a scene straight out of *Mr. Bean*.

"Wisha wausha camera pisha?" he persisted.

"One?" I said hoping that was the right answer.

"You aren't Sri Lankan. Are you?"

"Shit. How could you tell?

"Well for starters they know more Sinhala than 'Ow' and also they don't stop at the ticket counter, they just wave and drive in. Now please pay 2920 SLR per person."

"Curses, foiled again! Muttley, do something!" Sri exclaimed and looked at Sam. I suppose it was worth a shot. At least we got a laugh out of that disaster.

The trail circuit was eight kilometres long and it was completely foggy. We had to wait for thirty minutes at World's End to catch the view, but it was definitely a sight to see. A five hundred metre sheer drop with another three hundred metres at a slight gradient to the bottom; it would probably be a dream spot for base jumpers or wing-suiters. As expected, it did not lead to *Patal Lok,* not that we were in any hurry to get there.

Our next stop was at the Hakgala Gardens or *Ashoka Vatika.* This was the place where Ravana kept Sita Devi prisoner, as Queen Mandodari would not allow her to be brought into the royal palace. This was also the place, where Lord Hanuman first met Sita Devi and passed to her, Lord Rama's ring. There were thousands of species of plants and hundreds of butterflies flying around. In the spring season, the gardens were supposed to look their best with all the plants in full bloom; unfortunately for us that was a long way off.

A short while later, we were at the Sita Amman temple – the place where Sita Devi had a shower during her captivity. All I can say for the place was that it was beautiful – the stream, thick vegetation with Ashoka trees, and the peaks perfectly complemented the dust and smoke raised by the dozens of tourist vehicles. There are also some holes of varying sizes in the ground near the river, which were *apparently* the footprints of Lord Hanuman; the varying sizes were indicative of how he grew bigger in size.

As I sat in the corner of the temple, a little girl walked over and gave me some of her *Prasad* along with a huge smile. It was very kind of her and it struck me how children can be so innocent and trusting. My misanthropy went into overdrive and reminded me of the dangers and grim consequences that had been drilled into my head far too many times. I wanted to scream at the little girl, tell her that the world wasn't a safe place, that there were real monsters out there that she should stay close to the safety of her family, but I didn't. Why is a good question?

After receiving her kindness, who was I to destroy her innocence, her unquestioning belief in goodness? Was I a guardian and of what? If anything, I had to guard that, the part of humanity's divinity I had just experienced.

It certainly wasn't that reason alone. It was also because I was selfish. I wanted to see that innocence for longer, the faith in humanity. It made me forget my problems and my fears. It was something that I had lost a long time back and the loss had left me jaded. Why would I want to do that to someone else?

I realised that I was nothing at that moment, but the doubt that haunts all of humanity; the one that makes us think before smiling at a stranger; the one stops us from saying a kind word or extend a helping hand. It had to die; I had to kill it and now was the time.

I was thinking about this when we met her family – a large group of warm, kind, and friendly people. For some reason they were excited that we were from India or as they put it – the land of Shahrukh Khan, and invited us to have lunch at their place the next day. We politely declined their offer as we had a long way to go and bid them farewell.

While the incident in itself was trivial, something that I would have brushed aside on any normal day of my life, in that situation, it affected me a lot. It is hard to explain, but there are these experiences – the ones at exactly the right place and the right time. They could be as small as a stranger's words, a line in a book, and a dialogue from a movie or as large as an accident, but these are the ones that change our lives and define who we are.

Humanity 5, Misanthropy 2, and Dogeism 3.

No questions asked. I knew clearly what I wanted to believe in and certainly didn't need the scoring anymore. What Sam was thinking of though, I couldn't tell. He would have to make his own choice.

Day 70: Fear of the Dark

Location: Nuwara Eliya, Sri Lanka

Our first visit of the day was to the Divurumpola temple, located five kilometres from Welimada. Legend has it that Sita Devi performed the 'Agni Pariksha' at this place and there is a temple there to mark the spot. The kind monk, who was in charge of the place explained that the word *Divurumpola,* itself meant 'place of oath' in Sinhala. He also mentioned that the Bodhi tree present in the complex was a descendant of the sapling of the Sri Maha Bodhi. After we visited the temple and offered our prayers, he insisted that we had our breakfast there. After the previous day's experience, I had an open heart and the monk only helped the experience. It was true what Sri said, the world really was a good place with plenty of kind people.

Humanity 6, Misanthropy 2, and Dogeism 3.

The road from Welimada to Banderwela was one of the best roads in Sri Lanka and felt like heaven to us after having driving upon some of the roads and non-roads. It offered all that we could have wished for – beautiful views, plenty of curves, flat straights, clear road signs, and very little traffic. Banderwela was the place, where Lord Hanuman was supposed to have first landed in Sri Lanka after leaping from Mahendragiri.

We looked around for a sign but didn't find anything relevant. One of the major hassles that we had on the trip was the difficulty in locating smaller or lesser-known tourist spots. For example on the road to Ella, we saw a sign pointing to a viewpoint. Theoretically, it was supposed to be one and a half kilometres away. Practically, it was impossible to locate despite seeking directions from half a dozen locals. This wasn't a one off case either, over the duration of the trip, we had failed to "find" a stone bridge, a stone temple, some ruins, and multiple other places that had signs on the main road and no follow up signs whatsoever. If they were taking the trouble of putting up a sign on the main road, they might as well have put up a couple of follow up signs.

It could have been a devious ploy by the tourism department though; one from which our tourism department could take a page out of to boost their revenues – just stick a random sign pointing off a highway – 'Great wall of India – 2 kilometres', 'Leaning tower of Chital', 'Hanging gardens of Cham Cham' and enjoy a steady stream of revenue. Be creative in abusing people's intelligence considering that if people can't find them, it's because **they are** morons.

A little later, we reached the Ravana temple near Ella and were disappointed to find that the temple did not contain an idol of Ravana. The guardians of the temple directed us to the Ravana caves, which were about five hundred metres uphill from the temple.

Legend has it that Ravana built this cave network, which extended across Sri Lanka. Their purpose was to connect various locations of his empire and serve as a secret means for espionage, reconnaissance, and escape. The entrance to the cave was huge and so was the main chamber of the cave. There were three tunnels from the main chamber, tunnel one, which was the largest, ended after twenty feet, tunnel two, ended after ten feet, and tunnel three, which was the smallest didn't seem to have an ending.

After a bit of cave exploration, we visited the Ravana falls, which were beautiful. The only problem was the throng of idiots at the falls. "Hey, look there are lots of tourists here to appreciate the beauty of the place and they are taking pictures as well. You know what we should do to enhance their experience. Yes, you guessed right – pull out the shampoo packets, it's time for a game of strip and shampoo." There were a dozen men standing in their underwear, shampooing, coolly staring into the cameras of the tourists, who were desperately trying to take a *safe for work* picture of the falls. Disappointed, we headed to Arugam Bay.

Day 71: When I say it doesn't hurt me that means I can bear it.

Location: Arugam bay, Sri Lanka

There is no experience more humbling than lying on a flimsy wooden board with the ocean below you. You realise how truly insignificant you really are and feel completely overwhelmed by its vastness. However, there is also a lesson to be learnt – there might be a multitude of things out there beyond your control, yet to succeed, you have to cast your doubts aside and paddle forward for that elusive wave, the one that will change everything, the one that will make all the troubles worth it.

It is easy to stay still, the warm sun on your back keeps away the cold of the ocean and makes it oh so easy to sit there and do nothing but enjoy the moment, eventually though you have to take the plunge. To stay still is to stagnate, to sink, and eventually perish. Whatever the choice, the experience is still unique for each individual, either deeply philosophical or a pure unadulterated adrenaline rush, alternating between both, depending on whether you are waiting for a wave or surfing one.

This quote from surfer Gary Sirota pretty much summed up our whole trip, *"There are no more committed people on the planet than surfers. We fall down a lot. We turn around, paddle back out, and do it over and over again. Unlike anything else in life, the stoke of surfing is so high that the failures quickly fade from memory."*

Our next destination was Ussanagoda – one of the cities of Ravana's kingdom that Lord Hanuman burnt down. As usual, there were no signboards and after a few failed attempts at finding the place, a kind soul took pity on us and gave us precise directions, "Take a left off the highway near the factory, follow the road, and take a walk when it ends near the cliffs." We followed his directions to the T and got lost. My internal compass was broken beyond repair and was probably less functional than a suicidal lemming; at least they could find the edge of the cliffs.

Thankfully, after an hour of searching, we ran into a kid who led us to Ussanagoda. Thick shrubbery surrounded the three kilometre circular plain and the soil was red in colour. No shrubbery grew in the plain though, supposedly due to the fire that burnt down the place. Scientifically, you could say that it was because of the high iron levels in the soil. Some of the legends were definitely more believable than the rest.

We headed towards Galle and along the way visited the blowhole at Unnawaya and the Buddha statue at Matale, which was supposed to be one of the tallest in Lanka. Once in Galle, we drove to the old fort area on Peddlar's street and got a room at *Khalid's*.

Day 72: Revelations

Location: Galle, Sri Lanka

We were up early in the morning and took a walk around the fort, where we found a few locals jumping off the battlements of the Galle fort into the sea. It looked like fun and soon we were jumping off the walls as well. A quick shower later, we went back to exploring the fort and later headed towards Rumassala, a small hill near Galle. The hill is believed to be a piece of the *Rishabha* Mountain, which Lord Hanuman had brought to Lanka during the Ramayana war. Pieces of the mountain are said to have fallen off at several places in both India and Sri Lanka. Rumassala and Sirumalai were just a couple of these places that we had visited.

This was the final place to visit in our journey. We spent some time sitting in the temple, thinking about the last few months. None of us uttered a word; we just sat there, silently. Eventually, we started driving to Colombo. It was the end of an adventure and time for us to head back home. The end of a trip always was a mixed bag of emotions for us. We would feel happy to be heading home, with a bunch of experiences to share with family and friends. At the same time, the realisation that we were going back to our normal lives and that we wouldn't be seeing new places or having new experiences would be depressing.

This time however that wasn't the case. We had come to understand that we could be equally happy if we started Operation Random Monkey Adventures. We didn't need a big-bang vacation to have fun; we could spend weekends or even a weekday going on random smaller trips. The trick was *not to plan* too much and just head out.

Adventurer, Bruce Kirkby put it wisely when he said that we were forgetting the true spirit of adventure. We tend to focus on how long it is, how extreme the trip is, how many places we visit, or even on the gear but that isn't what it is.

"Adventure is curiosity, the willingness to embrace uncertainty, wondering about the possibility of doing just one thing differently, than before." - Bruce Kirkby, 'The Questions We Ask.'

It was a simple as that. We needed those tiny adventures in our boring city lives, to make us feel alive and inject freshness into our humdrum existence.

After plenty of stops along the beach, we eventually arrived in Colombo late in the evening and headed out to eat.

Day 73: Just because I am alone, does not mean I am lonely. I am not you.

Location: Colombo, Sri Lanka

To finish the trip successfully, we had to go through one final challenge, one that would stretch our limits and challenge us like nothing else had on this trip so far. Something that would break our mind, ravage our bodies, and claim our very souls – we had to do some shopping for the family! We decided to pick up some handicrafts at a place called 'Lakasala'. Most of the handicrafts in the shop were available in India as well, the exceptions being the *secret boxes* and the Sri Lankan style wooden masks and puppets.

After a ridiculous amount of shopping, I packed all the bags onto the *Baja* and started driving towards Negambo. It was time to return the motorcycles and we drove as slowly as possible. I had grown attached to the *Baja* and was definitely going to miss her a lot. Breaking up was such hard business, especially with the love of my life! I reached 'Sha Lanka' and handed her over to Suranga. It was time to head back home. Not like there was a choice, at the end of the day, home is where the heart is. We had friends to meet, stories to tell, and memories to relive.

That evening, we sat on the beach, reminiscing over incidents that took place in the last few months and how they had affected and changed us. Over the next couple of hours, we met a kite-surf cover maker, an Under-19 football player, a diver, and a gender challenged person. We exchanged stories about our lives, our families, and of the beauty of Sri Lanka. All the people who walked over asked me how I was, whether I was safe, and if I needed any help. They were all quite friendly and seemed to be concerned about my safety and wellbeing. It was quite ironic, considering that Sam was expecting us to get mugged or worse killed.

"So that's a +2 at the least, I guess. It's now **Humanity 8, Misanthropy 2, and Dogeism 3**. It's clear what the world is like Sam. Heck, even Dogeism has done better. Time to accept the facts and get rid of your distrust."

"It ain't over yet bitch. We aren't back home yet."

"So you actually want something to go wrong just to prove a point."

"I don't. I know the reality of it. That's all."

"Did you die or get seriously injured?"

"No, but we lost a lot of money."

"We made a ton of friends, we have experienced things we wouldn't have if we were paranoid monkeys and we would have never had so much fun either."

"Just shut up till tomorrow, will ya."

"Always tomorrow, never today; that is how, lives waste away."

We headed back into town for dinner and that was when we met an amazing man – a chubby, stoic, British law teacher. He had been teaching primarily in rural areas in Pakistan, India, and Sri Lanka for the last ten years for nearly no pay. As we ate, he told us his story. Teaching was his passion and he believed that was what would make the world a better place. He had been teaching in Pakistan for a few years where he received death threats for his work. Following a few unfortunate events, he was forced to leave Pakistan. He decided to continue pursuing his dream and moved to Sri Lanka. Every morning he would cycle to a faraway village to teach and would return at night. I found it extraordinary that a man would be willing to risk his life and sacrifice so much for strangers.

Men like these are the ones who give you hope about humanity and inspire us to have faith. Ironically, I didn't even know his name. It wasn't his name that mattered though, it was his commitment and conviction towards making the world a better place.

"So, what do you have to say now? It's the end and nothing went wrong," Sri said.

"This time," was Sam's reply.

"Every time. We drove all over Sri Lanka, walked across India and nothing went wrong. If you keep expecting things to go wrong you will never trust anybody and will lose out on a lot in life. This is how it will play out, every single time."

"Nothing?"

"In the grand scheme of things, it was nothing. We came out way ahead thanks to how much help we received from strangers so it's time to accept the world for what it is."

"Fine, I'll give it a shot. Happy now, Mother," Sam said in his usual manner.

Just then, a person walking by looked at me and asked, "Excuse me. Are you talking to me?"

"No. I was just talking to my..." I looked around at the empty beach, smiled at him, and walked away.

All we are is a collection of thoughts.

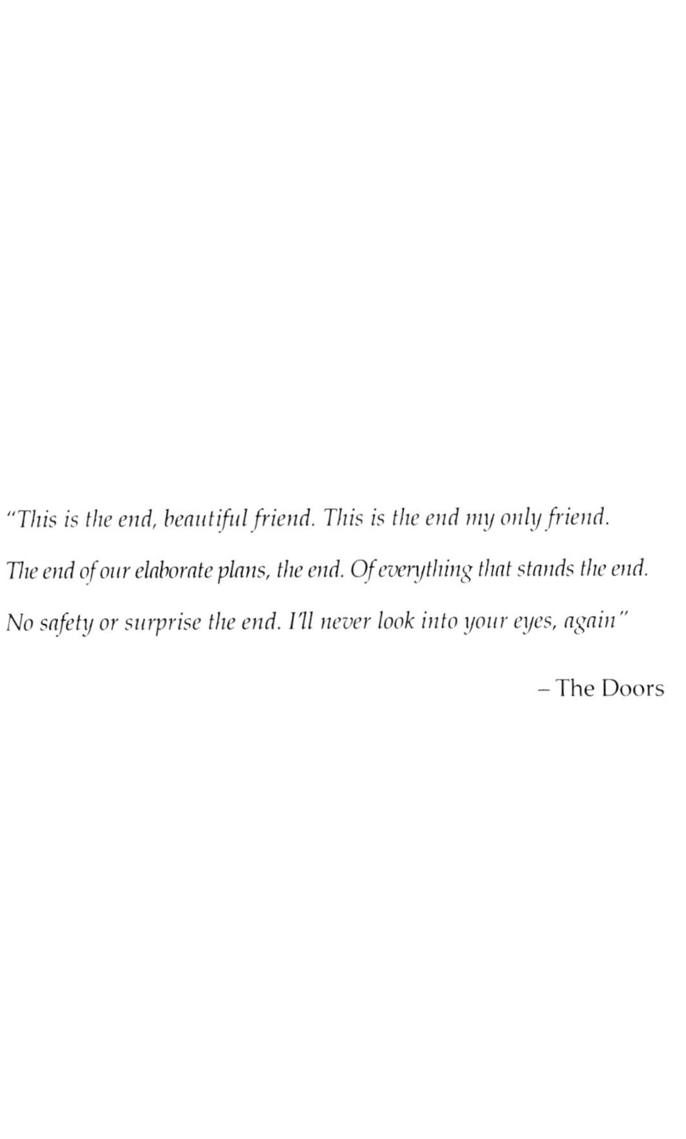

"This is the end, beautiful friend. This is the end my only friend.

The end of our elaborate plans, the end. Of everything that stands the end.

No safety or surprise the end. I'll never look into your eyes, again"

– The Doors

Acknowledgements

When I think about it, the number of people who have influenced this journey and in turn *MMM* is staggering. There is no way I could possibly thank all of them for everything they have done for me, but I am going to take a shot at it anyway.

I would begin by offering my prayers to Lord Hanuman, for the dream and the strength to pursue it, and for everything, he has given me in life. My deepest gratitude to my grandparents and parents for making me the person I am, in spirit and in person. My parents, for being supportive and encouraging in their own weird way, especially while I was on the journey. (Yes Dad, your tantrums helped!) My grandparents, for watching over me and keeping me safe. (I know you are watching.) My family for all the good advice and the on-call support. (See, I didn't die and look no loss of limbs either!)

My thanks to Ram and Sri for being the most patient 'Home Base' that a directionally challenged person could hope for and for motivating me to work on *MMM*. (I still swear you said four right turns at the lake.) The Bear, the Fox, the Tiger, and the Bandicoot for keeping me updated on all the trek routes, for getting me permits for forest sections, and more importantly for keeping me on track and giving me better things to focus on rather than on walking the distance. ("Go ahead, do it, it will be a walk in the park", they said. Yeah, right!) To all my friends, the deep conversations that we have had, have changed me and worked themselves into *MMM*. (No lawsuits for plagiarism, please!)

My cousins, who constantly called and kept me motivated through the trip. Without your constant encouragement, I couldn't have made it through to the end. ("No, I was not stabbed and no, I am not dying. Do not get on the damn plane!")

I am indebted to all the strangers I encountered along the way who spared a smile, a kind word, and much more. Even though at times, I didn't understand a word they said, the thought helped me take those few extra steps forward. A sincere bow to the holy men and enlightened souls, who helped me understand what faith was and how the world worked. My heartfelt gratitude also goes to the guides, fellow travellers, and strangers, who walked me through various religious and historical sites and helped me understand their history, importance, and the stories and legends that were associated with them. The dogs that walked along with me with absolutely no expectations; thanks for your selflessness and good cheer. (No, not the one who tried to hump my bag.)

A special thanks to my friend Bear, for helping me edit the book to the stage of publication. Thanks also goes to Major Srikanth for believing in *MMM* and pushing me to approach Leadstart. I am also thankful to the good folks at Leadstart Publishing, Mr. Swarup Nanda, Ms. Cora Bhatia, and the design and marketing teams for believing in *MMM* and helping me refine it to the point of publication.

Last but not the least, thanks to Sam and Sri, for understanding and going along with my insanity. What more could I ask for in friends. Maybe a little less snarkiness from Sam and a little less self-righteousness from Sri! However, in all seriousness, it was all possible only thanks to both of you. (Now let's go plan the next big trip!)

About the Author

Harsha is a freelance writer and the author of 'Monkeys, Motorcycles, and Misadventures'. After graduating with a Master's in Business Administration, he worked with a large IT company for a few years, before taking a sabbatical to trek the *Hanuman route*. In 2013, he moved to a beach town, where he spent a year beach bumming, mooching off family, and writing 'Monkeys, Motorcycles, and Misadventures'. For photographs, maps, and additional information about MMM, please visit the Facebook page: https://www.facebook.com/monkeysmotorcyclesandmisadventures or the MMM website: www.monkeysmotorcyclesandmisadventures.com

References

Given below is a list of books, articles, and websites that I referred to while writing this book. Points 4 to 14 specifically refer to material on the location of Lanka and the route that Lord Hanuman might have taken. Various other material related to the places visited along the route have also been included in the references. In addition to the above listed material, various guides, priests, monks, forest officials, and both the Indian and Sri Lankan tourism departments provided a lot of information about the route and places associated with Lord Hanuman and the Ramayana.

1. "Grandma Gatewood" one of the first Ultralight backpackers who had hiked through the entire Appalachian Trail (2168 miles) at the sprightly age of 67 years. http://www.witf.org/hiking-midstate-pa/2012/06/the-2012-class-of-the-appalachian-trail-hall-of-fame.php
2. Ray Jardine, *Beyond Backpacking: Ray Jardine's Guide to Lightweight Hiking.* (AdventureLore Press, 1999)
3. The Mountaineers, *Mountaineering: The Freedom of the Hills.* (Mountaineers Books, 2010)
4. "Historicity Of The Era Of Lord Rama" http://serveveda.org/documents/Historicity_era_of_lord_Rama.pdf
5. *Srimadvalmeekiya Ramayana* (Geeta Press, Gorakhpur)
6. Dr. Ram Avtar, *Shri Rama Van Gaman Sthal.* (Shri Rama Sanskritik Shodh Sansthan Trust, New Delhi)
7. Rama Sethu, (Rameswaram Rama Sethu Protection Movement, Chennai)
8. Joseph E. Schwartzberg, *Historical Atlas of South Asia*
9. "Places in the Ramayana"http://en.wikipedia.org/wiki File: Places RelatedToRama.JPG
10. Edward Moor, *The Hindu Pantheon.* (Asian Educational Services, New Delhi)
11. V.H Vader, *The Indian Historical Quarterly Vol II*
12. M.S. Purnalingam Pillai, *Ravana - The Great King of Lanka.* (Asian Educational Services, New Delhi)

13. Sirdar M V Kibe, *Location of Lanka.* First Edition (Monohar Mohadeo Kelkar, 1947)
14. R.L. Gupta, *The Antiquity of Rama's Era, Prachya Pratibha* (Prachya Niketan, Vol. 11-1, 1982[?])
15. Valmiki Ramayana, *Kishkindha Kanda, Sarga* 40, 41, 42
16. Livingstone Ian, *Dicing with Dragons.* (Routledge, 1982)
17. Gary Alan Fine, *Shared Fantasy.* (University of Chicago Press, 2002) pp. 17. ISBN 0-226-24944-1
18. "Official Website of Mysore Palace Board, Karnataka, India" http://www.mysorepalace.gov.in/index.htm
19. "Geographical Location of the Cave Networks"http://ancient voice.wikidot.com/article:maya-in-ramayana#toc8
20. "There Are Other Rivers" http://www alastairhumphreys.com/ books/thereareotherrivers/
21. "The Golden Chariot (Thanga Thēr)" http://palani.org/golden_chariot.htm
22. Ramanathaswamy Temple, *22 Holy Theertha's, Its Greatness and Speciality.* (Temple Publications, Rameswaram,2006)
23. Arulmigu Ramanathaswamy Temple, *A Guide Book of Rameswaram-Dhanushkodi.* (Arulmigu Ramanathaswamy Temple, Rameswaram, 2010)
24. "Arishadvargas"http://en.wikipedia.org/wiki/Arishadvargas
25. "Jain monastery at Kazhugumalai", The Hindu, Wednesday, 20 July 2011, http://www.thehindu.com/todays-paper/tp-features/ tp-editorialfeatures/article2260793.ece
26. Dept. of Tourism and District administration, Tirunelveli under Western Ghats, *Tourist Guide, Tirunelveli.* (Co-op., press, Thootukudi)
27. "Homepage of Kalugumalai" http://www.kalugumalai.com/
28. J Agarwal, *I am proud to be a Hindu.* (Hindoology Books, 2008)
29. Swami Harshananda, *All About Hindu Temples.* (Sri Ramakrishna Math, Chennai, 2011)
30. Devdutt Pattanail, *Sita: An illustrated retelling of the Ramayana.* (Penguin Books, India, 2013) ISBN 9780143064329
31. "Temple for Kethu dedicated to Siva at Mannar", The Hindu, Friday, 06 December 2002, http://hindu.com/thehindu/ fr/2002/12/06/stories/2002120601140600.htm

32. Sir Kanthiah Vaithianathan, *Thiruketheeswaram Papers*. (Sivanantha Kurukulam Thiruketheeswaram Temple Restoration Society, Colombo, 2003)
33. B. Sivaramakrishna Sarma, Śrī Munnesvara Varalaru [The History of Śrī Munnesvaram Temple]. (The Colombo Co-operative Printers› Society Ltd., Colombo,1968)
34. "UNESCO: Sacred City of Anuradhapura" http://whc.unesco.org/en/list/200
35. "Ruwanweliseya Stupa (144 BC), Anuradhapura", Riolta Sri Lankan Holidays. http://www.mysrilankaholidays.com ruwanweliseya.html
36. "The History of Buddhism", Dr. C. George Boeree, http://webspace.ship.edu/cgboer/buddhahist.html
37. "MIHINTALE: The cradle of Buddhism in Sri Lanka" http://www.lankalibrary.com/heritage/mihintale.htm
38. "Mihintale: Where Buddhism Blossomed in Sri lanka" http://www.srilankaview.com/Mihintale.htm
39. Clarke, Arthur C, *The Reefs of Taprobane; Underwater Adventures around Ceylon*. (Harper, New York, 1957) ISBN 0-7434-4502-3
40. "Worship of gods in Sri Lanka", Sunday Observer, Sunday, 4 March 2012, http://www.sundayobserver.lk/2012/03/04/imp04.asp
41. Sacred Island, A Buddhist Pilgrim's Guide to Sri Lanka by Ven.S.Dhammika
42. Jayasinghe Balasooriya, *The Glory of Ancient Polonnaruwa*. (Parakum Books, Polonnaruva, 2004) ISBN 955-8158-01-1
43. Central Cultural Fund, *World Heritage Site of Sigiriya*. (Central Cultural Fund Press)
44. "UNESCO: Ancient City of Sigiriya" http://whc.unesco.org/en/list/202
45. Professor Mangala Ilangasinha, *Dambulla Rock Temple*. (Rangiri Dambulla Development Foundation)
46. "UNESCO: Golden Temple of Dambulla" http://whc.unesco.org/en/list/561
47. "The Golden Temple Sri Lanka" http://www.goldentemple.lksite/
48. Guide Map, Royal Botanic Gardens, Peradeniya – Sri Lanka

49. "Elephants released under strict criteria", Sunday Observer, Sunday, 19 February 2012, http://www.sundayobserver lk /2012/ 02/19/fea09.asp
50. Chinmaya Mission of Sri Lanka, *Ramayana in Lanka.* (Chinmaya Mission of Sri Lanka, 2011) ISBN 978-955-8801-03-1
51. David Hatcher Childress, Ivan Terence Sanderson, Vimana Aircraft of Ancient India and Atlantis
52. Initial information was gathered through Google, Wikipedia and Lonely Planet

CPSIA information can be obtained at www.ICGtesting.com
Printed in the USA
LVOW11s1323051115

461239LV00004B/150/P